High Season

English for the Hotel and Tourist Industry

Workbook

Michael Duckworth

Oxford University Press

OXFORD
UNIVERSITY PRESS

Great Clarendon Street, Oxford OX2 6DP

Oxford University Press is a department of the University of Oxford.
It furthers the University's objective of excellence in research, scholarship,
and education by publishing worldwide in

Oxford New York

Auckland Cape Town Dar es Salaam Hong Kong Karachi
Kuala Lumpur Madrid Melbourne Mexico City Nairobi
New Delhi Shanghai Taipei Toronto

With offices in

Argentina Austria Brazil Chile Czech Republic France Greece
Guatemala Hungary Italy Japan Poland Portugal Singapore
South Korea Switzerland Thailand Turkey Ukraine Vietnam

OXFORD and OXFORD ENGLISH are registered trade marks of
Oxford University Press in the UK and in certain other countries

ISBN-13: 978 0 19 451310 4

Typeset by Tradespools Ltd, Frome, Somerset

Printed in China

ACKNOWLEDGEMENTS

The publishers and author would like to thank the following for their kind
permission to use articles, extracts or adaptations from copyright material:
Forte Leisure Breaks 1993 (p. 4 and Bloomsbury Hotel p. 66); Kuoni Travel
(p. 8); Trans Indus Ltd. (p. 50); David Churchill and *Business Life* ('Hotel
Update, p. 55); Bournemouth International Centre (p 59); Down Hall (p. 62);
Scandinavian Seaways (p. 64); *Pride of Britain* (Woolley Grange and Thornbury
Castle p. 66).

Cover photography by:
Tony Stone Images

Illustrations by:
Sharon Pallent/Maggie Mundv Illustrators' Agency (pp. 12, 50); Alex Tiani
(pp. 19, 28); Darrell Warner (pp. 30, 31, 40).

Location photography by:
Emily Anderson: Ander McIntyre.

We would also like to thank the following for their permission to reproduce
photographs:
Forte Hotels (p. 4 and Bloomsbury Hotel p. 66); Life File (Gatuguta Kararahe,
safari, p. 8; John Dakers, beach, p. 8; Mike Maidment, p. 38; Tim Fisher, gym,
p. 56); Travel Ink Photo Library (Abbie Encock, zebras, p. 8; David Toase, pony
trekking, p. 47; Abbie Enock, pool, p. 56); TRIP Photo Library (T. Mackie, p. 9;
W. Steer, shooting, p. 47); Hyatt Hotels (p. 55); Tony Stone Images (Robert
Evans, Castle hotel, p. 56; Bruce Ayres, business meeting, p. 56); Bournemouth
International Centre (p. 59); Down Hall Hotel (p. 62); Scandinavian Seaways
(p. 64); Thornbury Castle (p. 66); Woolley Grange Hotel (p. 66).

Contents

	page
Unit 1	4
Unit 2	10
Unit 3	16
Unit 4	22
Unit 5	28
Unit 6	34
Unit 7	40
Unit 8	46
Unit 9	52
Unit 10	58
Unit 11	64
Unit 12	70
Answer Key	76

Unit 1

Exercise 1   Read the descriptions of the three hotels. Then read what the three people say. Which hotel would each person prefer?

☆ FORTE CREST

Sipson Road, West Drayton, Middlesex, UB7 0JU

This modern hotel stands just off Junction 4 of the M4, and within easy reach of Heathrow by courtesy bus service and the Underground link to Central London. Royal Windsor and Hampton Court are both just a short trip from the hotel.

☆ 568 bedrooms & 4 suites ☆ 3 restaurants, including Chinese and Italian ☆ 2 bars ☆ lounge ☆ hair-drier, trouser press, overnight laundry service ☆ satellite TV ☆ 24-hour room service ☆ free car park ☆ use of local health and Fitness Centre ☆ FAMILY: baby-sitting, notice required; play area

£54
p.p.p.n.

THE WALDORF

Aldwych, London WC2B 4DD

Recently restored to its original Edwardian splendour, this elegant hotel stands on the crescent of Aldwych, where London's West End meets the City, and just on the fringe of Covent Garden. Built in 1908, its famous Palm Court Lounge retains the gracious ambience of the

turn of the century, and is the setting for tea dances. Shops, museums, and theatres are within walking distance, and Covent Garden Underground station is on hand.

☆ 262 bedrooms & 30 suites ☆ Waldorf Restaurant; Aldwych Brasserie ☆ Club Bar; Footlights Bar ☆ Palm Court Lounge ☆ hair-drier, trouser press, individually controlled air-conditioning ☆ satellite TV ☆ 24-hour room service ☆ public pay car park in vicinity ☆ Family: baby-sitting, notice required.

From **£79**
p.p.p.n.

GROSVENOR HOUSE APARTMENTS

Park Lane, London W1A 3AA

Built in 1928, the Grosvenor House Apartments were originally designed as a separate block of luxury service apartments on Park Lane. Incorporated into the main hotel one year later, the Apartments have been since, and are today, one of London's most prestigious and comfortable addresses. The Apartments are served by a private entrance and separate reception, resulting in unusual privacy and tranquillity, as well as an unrivalled level of service from the dedicated Apartments staff and management. Ranging in size from one to five bedrooms, ideal for families, the Apartments all have a spacious sitting-room, bathroom, hall, and kitchenette. All the hotel facilities are close at hand and included within the rate, such as the Health Club with its 65-foot swimming-pool and gymnasium. Children under 16 stay free in their own room.

From **£139**
p.p.p.n.

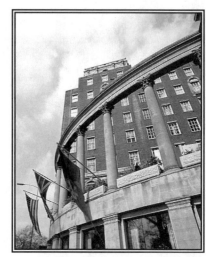

'I work for one of the large tour operators, so I spend most of my time travelling. In my opinion, hotels need to be efficient; the phones should work and there should be an overnight laundry service. I think a good range of restaurants is important, because I don't have time to go out in the evening. As far as I'm concerned, atmosphere isn't very important.'

a Jenny Wright would like the _____

'We have a small family business in Spain, and when we travel to England on business we like to take the children with us. I don't think the big hotels look after small groups very well – they often put you on different floors, and you can only see each other in the restaurant. On the other hand, self-catering apartments aren't very good because there aren't enough facilities. If you ask me, there should be more hotels that offer a mixture of both facilities.'

b Miguel Morales would like the _____

'I don't travel to London very often, but I sometimes go for the weekend. For me, the ideal hotel needs to be near the theatres and cinemas. If you ask me, the best hotels are old-fashioned ones with a lot of atmosphere, but of course they should have a good range of facilities too. For me, staying in a modern hotel would be an unpleasant experience.'

c Agatha Trump would like the _____

Exercise 2

Match the phrases in column A with the phrases in column B. The first one has been done for you.

A	B
1 _g_ I get terribly seasick, so I hate	**a** getting the chance to speak them.
2 __ Good service is important, but I dislike it	**b** welcoming the guests.
3 __ I go abroad whenever I can. I'm not fond	**c** staying in five-star hotels.
4 __ I'm not very keen	**d** getting up early.
5 __ When the company's paying for them, I love	**e** smaller ones more.
6 __ I like working in Reception because I enjoy	**f** when waiters don't leave you alone.
7 __ Big hotels are OK, but I like	**g** going anywhere by boat.
8 __ I start work at six. I don't mind	**h** on visiting historical sites.
9 __ I speak three languages so I like	**i** of holidays in England.

Exercise 3   Fill the gaps in these sentences, using the words in brackets.

Examples:
(like) I *like* big hotels.
(enjoy/stay) I *enjoy staying* in big hotels.
(love/when) I *love it when* I get the chance to stay in big hotels.

a   (like) I _____ Italian restaurants.

b   (enjoy/go) I _____ to foreign countries.

c   (hate/travel) I _____ by boat.

d   (dislike/when) I _____ I have to stay in noisy hotels.

e   (can't stand) I _____ people who complain in restaurants.

f   (enjoy) I _____ good food.

g   (don't mind/when) I _____ the service is slow.

h   (love/stay) I _____ in bed late.

i   (don't like/when) I _____ the bill is wrong.

Exercise 4   **1**   Choose the phrase in italics which is grammatically correct.

Example:
I *don't like it when/can't stand* getting up early.

a   I *love it/am keen on* when I get the chance to go abroad.
b   I *am not very fond/dislike* of foreign food.
c   I *am quite keen/enjoy* on learning new languages.
d   I *don't mind it when/enjoy* meeting new people.
e   I *can't stand it when/hate* guests who complain all the time.

2   Now write five sentences using your own ideas and the phrases in italics which you did NOT choose in Part 1.

Example:
I don't like it when the manager criticizes me.

a   _____

b   _____

c   _____

d   _____

e   _____

Exercise 5

A tour operator is describing two different hotels in Sri Lanka to a client. Put the sentences in the correct order (from 1 to 12). The first one has been done for you.

a __ Right, well, there are two hotels that we usually recommend and they are the Oberoi, which is in Colombo itself, and the Ivory Inn.

b __ I'm not sure, really. Could you tell me a bit about the first one?

c __ Is the Ivory Inn more or less the same?

d __ Good afternoon. I'm planning to go to Colombo in Sri Lanka and I'd like some information about the hotels you recommend.

e _1_ Good afternoon, May's Travel. Claire Newton speaking. How can I help you?

f __ Yes, please. My name's John Stevens, and the address is 11 London Road, Cambridge.

g __ Is the Ivory Inn actually in Colombo, too?

h __ Thank you very much. Goodbye.

i __ No, it's very different. It's a private guest house, in fact, not a hotel. It's got twenty rooms with ceiling fans, and there are showers, but there's no hot water. It's very simple, really. Would you like me to send you the brochure?

j __ No, it's about seven miles away. What sort of hotel are you looking for?

k __ Yes, the Oberoi is a first-class hotel, with all the facilities you would expect. There's a good choice of restaurants, a pool, large grounds, tennis courts and so on.

l __ All right, Mr Stevens. I'll put that in the post this afternoon.

Exercise 6

The three words in the boxes on the outside can all be combined with one of the words in the box in the centre (e.g. *coffee shop, clothes shop, souvenir shop*). Match each combination. The first one has been done for you.

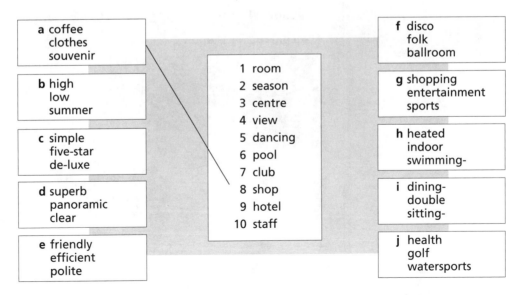

a coffee clothes souvenir		f disco folk ballroom
b high low summer	1 room 2 season 3 centre 4 view 5 dancing 6 pool 7 club 8 shop 9 hotel 10 staff	g shopping entertainment sports
c simple five-star de-luxe		h heated indoor swimming-
d superb panoramic clear		i dining- double sitting-
e friendly efficient polite		j health golf watersports

Exercise 7   Read the extract from the brochure and fill in the gaps with the following words. The first one has been done for you.

air-conditioned   relax
entertainment   rustic
facilities   setting
furnished   situated
informal   spacious
lies   value

Tradewinds

Tradewinds is [1] *situated* in [2]_____ grounds on the south coast at Diani, just over twenty miles from the city of Mombasa and within easy reach of some shops. It [3]_____ on a spectacular white-sand beach fringed by palm trees.

The main building is [4]_____ in style, with a thatched roof in the local African manner, and the hotel's [5]_____ include a restaurant, bar, hairdresser, and shop. By the swimming-pool is an [6]_____ snack bar and a smaller pool for children. Evening [7]_____ is provided by live bands or a disco.

The modestly [8]_____ rooms have a balcony or terrace, are fully [9]_____ , and have a telephone and shower.

Opinion: In a superb [10]_____ , this is a simple, medium-class hotel offering outstanding [11]_____ for money, and an ideal place to unwind and [12]_____ before going on safari.

Exercise 8   Answer the clues to find the hidden word. All the answers are connected
with accommodation. The first one has been done for you.

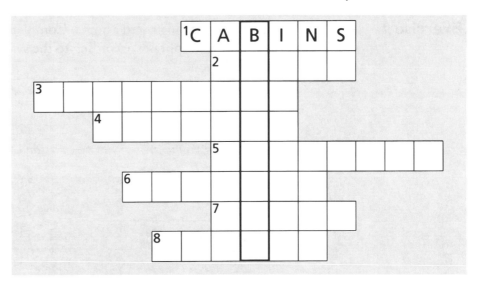

1 At the Yosemite Lodge you can stay in small redwood ___ . (6)
2 The millionaire reserved a ___ of six rooms on the top floor of the
   hotel. (5)
3 If you have a family, you should think about staying in a self-catering
   ___ that has three bedrooms, a kitchen, and a bathroom. (9)
4 At the Ahwahnee Hotel in Yosemite, you can rent a double room or a
   separate ___ in the grounds. (7)
5 We took our tents and stayed in a lovely ___ which had all the facilities
   we needed. (8)
6 We stayed in a marvellous hotel that even had ___ to keep your horse
   in. (7)
7 I'd rather stay in a five-star ___ than in a bed and breakfast. (5)
8 Our room doesn't have a bath, but at least there is a ___ . (6)

Unit 2

Exercise 1

A hotel guest is writing a letter home. Complete the letter by filling in the gaps with words or phrases according to the symbols. The first one has been done for you.

> I've just arrived at the hotel and tried to call you from the ☎
>
> ¹ telephone in my bedroom but as I couldn't get through, I thought
>
> I'd write you a letter instead. The room is really lovely - I've got my
>
> own ☐ ² _____ and I've just poured myself a gin
>
> and tonic from the 🍷 ³ _____ . It's all very civilized,
> M
>
> and even though it's nearly 30°C outside, the 📺 ⁴ _____
>
> _____ works really well. Tomorrow I thought I'd get up early
>
> and go down to the 🏊 ⁵ _____
>
> before breakfast, as I don't have to be at the meeting until 9.15.
>
>   We ought to think about coming here for a holiday. The hotel
>
> would be fine for the kids because 🐴 ⁶ _____
>
> and they could swim or 🎾 ⁷ _____ , and if
>
> the weather was bad, they could use the 🏓 ⁸ _____ .
>
> Apparently they also have 🌲 ⁹ _____ ,
>
> so we could even spend Christmas here. Anyway, I'll take some
>
> photos so you can see what it looks like.

Exercise 2

Complete the table on the next page with the following irregular verbs. Each verb can be used with one of the sets of words on the right. The first one has been done for you. Use a dictionary if you need to.

fly	ring
go	speak
know	spend
make	wear
pay	write

a	*make*	*made*	*made*	changes, a decision, a reservation
b	_____	_____	_____	on holiday, to bed, on a training course
c	_____	_____	_____	the bell, the fire alarm, room service
d	_____	_____	_____	first class, club class, economy class
e	_____	_____	_____	time, money, a holiday
f	_____	_____	_____	the bill, in cash, in advance
g	_____	_____	_____	someone well, the answer, a place
h	_____	_____	_____	English, French, quietly
i	_____	_____	_____	a uniform, clothes, a dinner jacket
j	_____	_____	_____	a letter, a fax, a message

Exercise 3

Put the verbs in these short dialogues into the correct form of the Simple Past. The first one has been done for you.

A: There's a message for you, Mr Smith.
B: Thank you. When [1]*did it arrive* (it/arrive)?
A: About an hour ago, sir.

A: Where [2]_____ (you/spend) your last holiday?
B: We [3]_____ (go) to the Canaries.
A: [4]_____ (you/have) a good time?
B: No, we [5]_____ (not/like) it very much. In fact, we [6]_____ (leave) a few days early.
A: What [7]_____ (you/not/like) about it?
B: We [8]_____ (think) it was much too modern.

A: I'm sorry, Mr Johnson, we don't seem to have a reservation for you. When [9]_____ (you/make) the booking?
B: I [10]_____ (not/write) to you myself – my secretary [11]_____ (fax) you last week. And she [12]_____ (send) a letter of confirmation too. She [13]_____ (book) it in the name of the company.
A: Oh yes, here it is. I do apologize.

Exercise 4   Look at the two pictures showing a bedroom at the Astron Hotel before and after renovation. Write sentences about what the new owners have done, using the Present Perfect, as in the example.

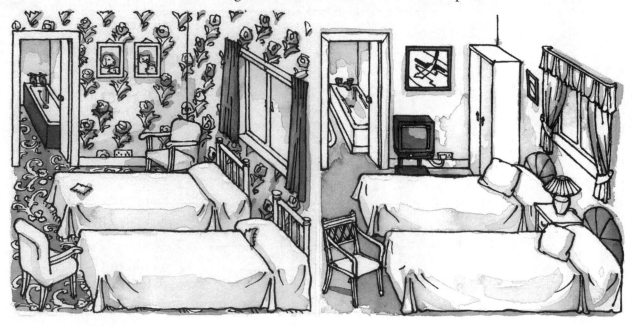

Example:
repaint/all/rooms
They have repainted all the rooms.

a put/new baths/all/bathrooms

_____

b replace/all/old beds

_____

c take down/old wallpaper

_____

d change/all/pictures

_____

e lay/new carpets

_____

f install/colour TVs/all/rooms

_____

g spend/a lot of money/curtains and fabrics

_____

h build/new cupboards/all/rooms

_____

Exercise 5

Read this extract from a tour operator's report about a visit to a hotel. Put the verbs into the Present Perfect or the Simple Past. The first one has been done for you. Use a dictionary if you need to.

REPORT: ASTRON HOTEL

We [1]*visited* (visit) the Astron Hotel in July 1991, when we [2]_____ (decide) that we would not feature the hotel in our brochure. There [3]_____ (be) a number of reasons for this: the rooms [4]_____ (need) upgrading, we [5]_____ (feel) that the standard of service [6]_____ (not/be) good enough, and the hotel [7]_____ (not/seem) to be well managed.

However, a great deal [8]_____ (change) since 1991, and the hotel is now under new management. They [9]_____ (redecorate) all the rooms and they [10]_____ (make) the restaurant much more comfortable and attractive. They [11]_____ (also/build) a new pool. They [12]_____ (start) work on a new extension which should be complete by April next year, and this will bring the number of available rooms to 200. The new manager [13]_____ (introduce) an incentive scheme for the staff, [14]_____ (increase) salaries, and [15]_____ (send) a number of employees on training courses, and as a result the level of service [16]_____ (improve) a great deal.

The restaurant is gaining a good reputation. The new chef, John White, [17]_____ (be) at the hotel for three months, and will clearly maintain high standards of cuisine. He [18]_____ (train) in Paris a few years ago, and then [19]_____ (work) at the Tour d'Argent. Since his arrival, he [20]_____ (create) a new menu and [21]_____ (hire) a new maitre d' to train the waiters. We [22]_____ (have) a meal at the restaurant last night and [23]_____ (think) the standards were excellent.

We therefore recommend that we feature the Astron Hotel in next year's brochure.

Exercise 6   Complete this table showing how to compare adjectives.

ADJECTIVE	COMPARATIVE	SUPERLATIVE
expensive	more expensive than	the most expensive
clean	_____	_____
_____	better than	_____
_____	_____	the cheapest
_____	more interesting than	_____
bad	_____	_____
_____	more spacious than	_____
_____	_____	the most comfortable
_____	bigger than	_____
_____	busier than	_____
quiet	_____	_____

Exercise 7   A potential guest is phoning a country house hotel to ask about differences between the rooms. Fill in the gaps with the comparative or superlative forms of the adjectives in brackets. The first one has been done for you.

HOTEL: Good afternoon, Carlton Court Hotel. How can I help you?

GUEST: Good afternoon. I'm phoning to ask about the three suites you feature in your brochure – the Nelson, the Clive, and the Drake. I'm trying to decide which one would be [1]*the most suitable* (suitable) for me. Are they all more or less the same?

HOTEL: No, they are all individually designed. I'll start with the Nelson suite – it has a single bed, a sitting-room and an en-suite bathroom. It costs £65 per night, so it's [2]_____ (cheap) of the three suites, but of course it is also [3]_____ (small) of the three because it's for one person.

GUEST: How much [4]_____ (big) are the other two?

HOTEL: About twice the size. The Clive is quite a lot [5]_____ (spacious) than the Nelson, and has a double bed, en-suite bathroom, a sitting-room, and a small dining-room. It's a little [6]_____ and costs £85 per night per person, but that does include dinner for two. It's the only suite on the top floor, so it has 7_____

(good) view of the city.

GUEST: And what is the Drake Suite like?

HOTEL: Well, it's £105 per person per night including dinner, so it's our

8_____ (expensive) suite, but it's also our

9_____ (popular) one, and reservations

need to be made well in advance. It is 10_____

(large) than either the Clive or the Nelson, and it's 11_____

(quiet) than them because it's at the back of the hotel.

GUEST: Thank you very much. I'll be in touch again soon.

Exercise 8

Complete the sentences by choosing a word from column A and a word from column B. The first one has been done for you.

A	B
play-	access
safety	size
stair	nurse
king-	rail
resident	bus
wheelchair	changing
nappy-	lift
courtesy	room

a   If the weather is bad, the children at the hotel can use the *play-room* on the ground floor.

b   In order to cater for guests who have babies, we have installed _____ _____ facilities in the toilets.

c   There's no need to get a taxi from the airport. We provide a _____ _____ .

d   Because many of our clients are elderly, we have a _____ _____ in case they need medical attention.

e   As the stairs are quite steep, we have fitted a _____ _____ .

f   One of the toilets on the ground floor has been widened to provide _____ _____ for disabled guests.

g   A number of our rooms now have _____ _____ beds as we have had complaints that the beds were too small.

h   We decided that the cheapest way of giving people in wheelchairs access to the first floor was to install a _____ _____ .

Unit 3

Exercise 1

Match the sentences in column A with the sentences in column B. The first one has been done for you.

A

1 d This is the third time you've been late.
2 __ They'll give you a tip if they want to.
3 __ I don't work in the Front Office.
4 __ It's nearly eight o'clock.
5 __ That sounded very rude.
6 __ The computer can work it out.
7 __ It's dangerous to change a light bulb like that.
8 __ Luckily all our guests are English.
9 __ You should always try to smile.

B

a You shouldn't stand and wait for one.
b I must get to work soon.
c We don't have to learn any other languages.
d You must get here on time.
e You should turn the light off first.
f Guests like it when receptionists are friendly.
g You mustn't speak to the guests like that.
h I don't have to wear a tie.
i You don't have to do the calculations yourself.

Exercise 2

In each of the following passages, choose one of the three words or phrases to fill the gaps. The first one has been done for you.

1 **must   don't have to   mustn't**

As it's your first day, I'll just show you what to do. Obviously, you ¹*must* make the beds and hoover the carpet, and you ²_____ forget to check the cupboards in case the guests have left anything. If one of the beds hasn't been used, you ³_____ change the sheets, but you ⁴_____ tidy it up so that it looks right. If the guest is about to leave, you ⁵_____ check the mini-bar and tell reception if anything has been used so that they can put it on the bill. In the bathroom, you ⁶_____ change all the towels and provide new soap and shampoo and make sure that everything is clean. If any of the light bulbs are broken, you ⁷_____ replace them yourself – you can just ring Maintenance and they'll take care of it.

2 **have to**   **don't have to**   **shouldn't**

The hotel is in the West End, so a lot of our guests want to go out to shows in London, and I [1]_____ try and arrange bookings for them. We have special arrangements with some of the cinemas and theatres, so that means our guests [2]_____ queue up for tickets and they [3]_____ pay more than they should, which is good for them. But with some of the others – especially the very popular musicals – we [4]_____ use agencies, and that means that the guests [5]_____ pay a lot extra. Personally I think that the agencies [6]_____ charge so much, but they always say that the guests [7]_____ make bookings at the last minute.

3 **should**   **don't have to**   **mustn't**

You [1]_____ know how to mix all the cocktails on the list, and you [2]_____ try and be as professional as possible, because that's all part of the atmosphere. Of course, you [3]_____ know how to make every cocktail in the world, because that would be impossible. If a guest asks you for a cocktail you don't know, you [4]_____ panic, you [5]_____ just ask them how to make it, and you [6]_____ show some interest in it because that makes them feel good. There are sometimes problems with people who are under age. If you think someone looks too young, you [7]_____ ask them for proof of their age and you [8]_____ serve them alcohol if they are under seventeen.

4 What jobs are described in the three passages above?

Passage 1 _____

Passage 2 _____

Passage 3 _____

Exercise 3   1   Complete the table of nouns and adjectives. The first one has been done for you. Use a dictionary if you need to.

NOUN	ADJECTIVE
a enthusiasm	*enthusiastic*
b _____	experienced
c friend	_____
d _____	able
e relevance	_____
f permanence	_____
g _____	responsible
h availability	_____
i _____	aware
j suitability	_____

2   Fill in the gaps in the following sentences using either the noun or the adjective in each pair in the table. The sentences are not in the same order as the table.

Example:
She'd be marvellous at organizing children's activities because she's got lots of *enthusiasm*.

a I'm rather shy and reserved, so I don't think a job in Reception would be _____ for me.

b Please send us a letter and a cv giving details of your qualifications and _____ experience.

c I'm surprised that she has decided to leave. I wasn't _____ that she wasn't happy here.

d If you want to work in Front Office, you have to develop the _____ to do three things at the same time.

e She is always happy, smiling, and _____ , so everyone likes her.

f I have several years' _____ of working in a large hotel.

g The Head Housekeeper is _____ for making sure that the rooms are kept in good condition.

h Could you phone Mr Peters and ask him when he would be _____ for the interview?

i I worked there on a three-month contract but I did well and at the end they offered me a _____ job.

Exercise 4

Choose a word from column A and a word from column B to complete the sentences. The first one has been done for you.

A	B
permanent	bedroomed
personal	clientele
kitchen	quarter
twelve-	rate
turnover	workload
regular	garden
winter	touch
heavy	staff

a   We have quite a high staff *turnover rate*. Our employees don't stay with us for very long.

b   We're fully booked in spring, summer and autumn, but the _____ _____ is very quiet.

c   We're a small family-run hotel, and our guests appreciate the _____ _____ that we offer.

d   We can't afford many staff, so the three of us who run the hotel have a _____ _____ .

e   We grow all our own herbs and vegetables in the _____ _____ .

f   Most of our guests come back again and again, so we have a fairly _____ _____ .

g   They run a large hotel that has over fifty _____ _____ and twenty other temporary employees.

h   My sister runs a small _____ _____ hotel with a small restaurant that is open to non-residents.

Exercise 5   Read the following advertisement. Choose one of the following words to fill the gaps. The first one has been done for you.

challenging	conference	Golf	opportunity
communication	essential	minimum	Personnel
competitive	experience	National	professional

MANOR HOUSE HOTEL AND GOLF COURSE

A magnificent Jacobean-style 69-bedroom hotel offering ¹*conference* facilities and its own Championship
²_____ Course, situated within a 270-acre country estate in the Dartmoor ³_____ Park.
We require a

DEPUTY HEAD RECEPTIONIST

A ⁴_____ opportunity has arisen to join our ⁵_____ and enthusiastic Front Office team.
You must possess excellent ⁶_____ and social skills coupled with a high level of guest care.
Computer experience is ⁷_____ , together with a ⁸_____ of 2 years' Front Office
⁹_____ .

In return we offer a ¹⁰_____ salary, live-in accommodation if required, and the ¹¹_____
to join one of Europe's most progressive hotel groups.

Please forward Curriculum Vitae to the ¹²_____ Manager, Priscilla Evans, the Manor House Hotel,
Moretonhampstead, Devon TQ13 8RE.

Exercise 6   Emma Jones has replied to the advertisement above. Complete her letter by choosing the best word or phrase from the options in italics. The first one has been done for you.

Dear Ms Evans

I am ¹*contacting/writing/talking* in reply to the advertisement for the ²*work/job/post* of
Deputy Head Receptionist which you ³*made/placed/wrote* in this month's edition of 'Caterer
and Hotelkeeper' magazine. I greatly enjoy working in a Front Office and taking
⁴*concern/care/attention* of guests, and would welcome the ⁵*possibility/occasion/opportunity*
to take on more responsibility by working for a much larger hotel.
    As you will see from the ⁶*enclosed/added/included* cv, I completed a course in Catering
and Hotel Management after ⁷*left/leave/leaving* school, and then worked part-time in a
number of hotels in London. ⁸*Since/For/At* the last year and a half I have been working
⁹*as/like/of* a receptionist in the Belmont Hotel, where I gained ¹⁰*valuable/expensive/costly*
experience of working ¹¹*with/of/from* computers and dealing with a wide range of guests.
    I also have a good working ¹²*understanding/ability/knowledge* of German and French, and I
also speak a ¹³*little/small/few* Italian. I would be ¹⁴*available/prepared/willing* for
interview from May 15th.

I look ¹⁵*ahead/up/forward* to ¹⁶*hearing/hear/heard* from you.

Yours ¹⁷*truly/sincerely/faithfully*

Emma Jones
Emma Jones

Exercise 7   Answer the clues to find the hidden word. The first one has been done for you as an example.

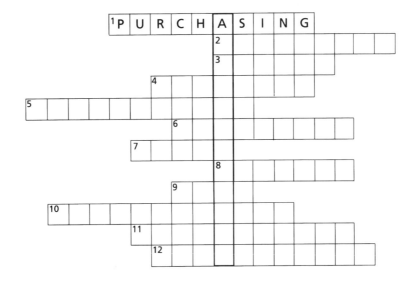

1 I work in the ___ Department – we are responsible for ordering and buying everything that the other departments need and for keeping control of stocks. (10)
2 Some large hotels have a ___ Officer who hires new employees, conducts interviews, and generally looks after the staff. (9)
3 There's no problem if you come back after midnight – the night ___ will let you in. (6)
4 In the ___ Department, we are responsible for paying bills and salaries, and for the financial side of the hotel. (8)
5 There's a vacancy for a ___ at the Medici Hotel – the job involves cleaning the guests' rooms, making the beds, and making sure that everything looks right. (11)
6 As a ___ , you will be expected to look after guests' special requests, and you'll have to make theatre bookings, organize tours, travel arrangements, and so on. (9)
7 I work in the ___ Office, so I deal directly with the guests, and for this kind of job you need to have good social skills. (5)
8 The General ___ has overall responsibility for the running of the hotel. (7)
9 The restaurant are looking for an experienced ___ with good pastry skills who can produce imaginative cuisine. (4)
10 I'm a ___ , so part of my job is to welcome the guests and give them their room keys; you need to have a friendly, outgoing personality for this kind of work. (12)
11 Peter is the head of the ___ Department, so contact him if you notice anything that needs repairing. (11)
12 The ___ is in charge of the cleaners and chambermaids, and is responsible for making sure that the rooms look as they should. (11)

Unit 4

Exercise 1

A guest is phoning the Marlow Hotel to book a room. Number the dialogue in the right order (1–14). The first one has been done for you.

a ___ American Express. The number's 8773 457 238 5549. Will you need a deposit?

b ___ Hello, I'd like to book a room, please.

c ___ Yes, it's Henry Box, and the address is 30 Lime Walk, Slough.

d ___ Certainly, sir. When would you like to come?

e ___ An individual booking – it's for our wedding anniversary.

f ___ No, but you've been recommended to us by friends.

g ___ I'll just check availability. Yes, that's fine. Is this a company booking or an individual booking, sir?

h ___ OK, 30 Lime Walk. May I ask if you've stayed with us before?

i ___ No, a deposit won't be necessary. If you'd like to make a note of your reservation number, it's P 227.

j _1_ Marlow Hotel, Reservations. Charles Thompson speaking.

k ___ That's nice to hear. How will you be paying?

l ___ Right, in that case we'll provide complimentary flowers and champagne. May I have your name, please?

m ___ On the eleventh of May, for two nights. A double room for myself and my wife.

n ___ Thank you very much. Goodbye.

Exercise 2

Use the information from the dialogue above to fill in this reservation card.

Reservation Card
Name
Arrival date
No. of nights
Room type
Company/Individual
Stayed before
Method of payment
Credit card no.
Address
Reservation no.

Exercise 3

Reply to the following questions using short answers.

Example:

Are there any lifts in the hotel? Yes, *there are.*

a It's a lovely day, isn't it? Yes, _____ .

b Excuse me, do you speak English? Yes, _____ .

c Do you work here? Yes, _____ .

d Is there a post-box anywhere here? Yes, _____ .

e Have you been here before? No, _____ .

f Are they going to stay another night? No, _____ .

g Have they confirmed that reservation? No, _____ .

h May I use your phone? Yes, _____ .

i Did you take his number? No, _____ .

j Have you got a pen I could borrow? Yes, _____ .

Exercise 4

Read through the information about some people who went to Spain. Then answer the questions, using short answers as in the example. Finally, work out which hotel everyone stayed in.

Peter, Mary, and the Smiths all went on holiday to Spain. They stayed in different hotels, the Granada, the Seville, and the Alhambra. Only two of the hotels were air-conditioned. Peter stayed in the only hotel with a pool. Each hotel had either air-conditioning or a pool. The Smiths did not stay in the Alhambra. The Granada did not have air-conditioning.

a Did Peter, Mary and the Smiths travel to Spain? *Yes, they did.*

b Did they stay in the same hotel? _____ .

c Were all three hotels air-conditioned? _____ .

d Did all the hotels have pools? _____ .

e Did Peter's hotel have a pool? _____ .

f Was Peter's hotel air-conditioned? _____ .

g Did the Smiths stay in the Alhambra? _____ .

h Could the Smiths have stayed at the Seville or the Granada?

_____ .

i Was the Granada air-conditioned? _____ .

j Did the Granada therefore have a pool? _____ .

Therefore, . . .

Peter stayed at the _____ .

The Smiths stayed at the _____ .

Mary stayed at the _____ .

Exercise 5   Match the following sentences with their question tags. The first one has been done for you.

1 <u>d</u> You've got a reservation,   a didn't they?
2 __ No one here speaks   b don't you?
     Japanese,   c wouldn't you?
3 __ I expect you want my   d haven't you?
     passport,   e have you?
4 __ This is a very nice hotel,   f do they?
5 __ You're leaving tomorrow,   g shall I?
6 __ I'll send you a letter of   h isn't it?
     confirmation,   i aren't you?
7 __ She's a very good   j isn't she?
     receptionist,
8 __ You haven't seen my pen
     anywhere,
9 __ They paid by credit card,
10 __ You'd like a room
     overlooking the garden,

Exercise 6   In the following telephone conversation, choose the correct option from the words in italics. The first one has been done for you.

HOTEL: Good morning, Landsdown Hotel. [1]*Can/Could* I help you?

GUEST: Good morning. Could I [2]*have/speak* Reservations, please?

HOTEL: Certainly. [3]*Wait/Hold* the line, please. I'll [4]*put/connect* you through.

GUEST: Thank you.

HOTEL: I'm sorry, [5]*I'm afraid/I regret* the line's busy. Will you [6]*hold/hang* on?

GUEST: Yes, that's [7]*fine/splendid*.

HOTEL: It's [8]*ringing/calling* for you now. . . . Reservations. Jane Watson [9]*talking/speaking*. How can I help you?

GUEST: Hello, [10]*this is/here is* Michael Nelson from Killick & Co. I rang earlier to book two singles from the 18th.

HOTEL: Yes, Mr Nelson, I remember. What can I [11]*do/make* for you?

GUEST: Could I change that to three singles, again from the 18th?

HOTEL: I'm [12]*afraid/sorry*, could you repeat that? It's a [13]*faint/bad* line.

GUEST: Yes, could I have another single room for the same dates?

HOTEL: Yes, [14]*obviously/of course*. I'll see to that now. I'd be [15]*grateful/delighted* if you could [16]*repeat/confirm* that in writing.

GUEST: [17]*Surely/Certainly*. Thank you for your help.

HOTEL: [18]*Your/You're* welcome. Goodbye.

Exercise 7   Find the words in the box to complete the sentences below. The words are hidden horizontally, vertically, and diagonally. The first one has been done for you.

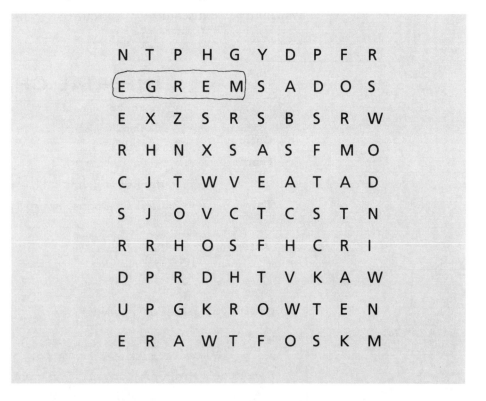

1 We have our guests' addresses on the computer, so it's easy to ___ them and send them a publicity letter. (5)
2 I find it difficult to read the words on the ___ because there's too much light behind it. (6)
3 You can work on different things at the same time – for example, you can work on two letters and use the calculator, and they all appear in different ___ . (7)
4 I don't use a typewriter any more – all our documents are done on the word-___ . (9)
5 I don't really like the way your letter looks – why don't you try doing it again in a different ___ ? (6)
6 We gather as much information about our guests as we can and we store the ___ on a hard disk. (4)
7 The new program makes it much easier to ___ the information that you need to find. (6)
8 Before you can get to the information about the hotel's finances, you have to type in a secret ___ . (8)
9 Our computers are linked together in a ___ so we can all exchange information. (7)
10 Whether or not a computer is easy to use depends on the ___ rather than the machine itself. (8)

Exercise 8   **1**   Fill the gaps in the fax with the following words. The first one has been done for you.

reserve	details	en-suite	following	Regards
availability	discount	Executive	including	single

IMPERIAL CHEMICALS

Date: 24 May

From: Miranda Smith,
                 Marketing and Promotions

To: Castle Lodge Hotel

Attention: Reservations

Could you please ^{1}*reserve* the ^{2}_____ rooms:

1 A single ^{3}_____ room for our Sales Director, Mr Henry Green, for two nights from August 18

2 A standard ^{4}_____ room with ^{5}_____ bathroom for our Sales Manager, Miss Caroline Lamb, for three nights from August 18

Please confirm ^{6}_____ and send ^{7}_____ of prices of rooms, ^{8}_____ half-board and our normal ^{9}_____ .

^{10} _____

Miranda Smith

Miranda Smith,
Manager

2   You work in Reservations at the Castle Lodge Hotel. The manager gives you the following instructions. Read them and complete the fax below.

'Could you send a fax to Imperial Chemicals? Thank them for the two bookings and say that'll be fine. You'd better quote the standard prices first, including half-board, service charges, and taxes – that's £165 and £85 a night. I think we usually give them 10% discount, so work out what it comes to and put the total at the end.'

CASTLE LODGE
HOTEL

Date: _____

From: Reservations

To: _____

Attention: _____

Thank you for_____

_____

_____

_____

_____

_____

_____

_____

_____

_____

_____

_____

_____

_____

_____

_____

_____

_____

_____

Unit 5

Exercise 1

Match the questions in American English in Column A with the replies in British English in column B. The first one has been done for you.

A

1 <u>d</u> Is there a drugstore downtown where I can get some diapers?

2 __ Where's the rest room?

3 __ Reception, the trash cans are all full.

4 __ I'm in a bit of a hurry. Can you get my check?

5 __ Did you have a vacation last year?

6 __ There's something wrong with the faucet in my room. Can you fix it?

7 __ Do you have a candy store in the hotel?

8 __ Do you have any potato chips?

9 __ Is there a gas station round here?

10 __ Are the prices any cheaper in the fall?

B

a Not exactly, but the souvenir shop has a range of sweets.

b Yes, we have a range of special autumn breaks.

c I am sorry. I'll send a plumber to mend the tap at once.

d Yes, there's a chemist called Boots in the city centre that has nappies.

e Yes, the nearest garage is just round the corner.

f Yes, I'll prepare your bill at once.

g No, I'm afraid we don't have any crisps, but we do have peanuts.

h The ladies' toilets are down the corridor on the left.

i Yes, I had a short holiday in Spain.

j I do apologize. I'll send someone to empty the bins at once.

Exercise 2

Some words have different meanings in American and British English. In each pair of sentences, one speaker is American and the other is British. Which is which?

Example:

I've lost my purse, and it's got my map book, passport, and make-up in it. *American*

I've lost my purse, and it's got my credit card and some small change in it. *British.*

a   I bought three pairs of pants, and they cost £2.50. _____

b   I bought three pairs of pants, and they cost £85.00. _____

c   I'm Jack, I'm twenty-one years old, and I go to school in Cambridge.
_____

d   I'm Jack, I'm fifteen years old, and I go to school in Cambridge.
_____

e   If we run out of gas, we'll just have to walk. _____

f   If we run out of gas, we'll just have to use the electric heater.
_____

g   If you want to get to the other side of the road, use the subway.
_____

h   If you want to get to the other side of the city, use the subway.
_____

i   I had a flat, but I decided to sell it. _____

j   I had a flat, so I got to the airport late. _____

Exercise 3

Put the following items of food into groups of three. The first two items have been done for you.

apple	leeks	rösti
béchamel	lyonnaise	salmon
broccoli	peas	sauté
haddock	plaice	tartare
ham	pork	veal

A	B	C	D	E
broccoli	_____	_____	_____	_____
peas	_____	_____	_____	_____
_____	_____	_____	_____	_____

Exercise 4   1   You are a waiter/waitress in a restaurant. Your customers want
explanations of different items on the menu. Answer their questions using
a phrase from each of the three columns.

A	B	C
a chicken breast	with a white stem	with garlic and cream.
a variety of shellfish	made with egg whites,	and a green top.
a kind of sweet	made with chocolate,	eggs and liqueur.
a kind of meat	made with milk,	and has pink flesh.
thinly sliced potatoes	that is quite large	but are much smaller.
a kind of sauce	filled with garlic butter,	young calves.
a very light dish	that look like lobsters,	vanilla, eggs and sugar.
a kind of fish	that comes from	and coated with breadcrumbs.
a kind of vegetable	that are baked	and baked in the oven.

Example:
What is Chicken Kiev?
It's a chicken breast filled with garlic butter and coated with breadcrumbs.

a   What are prawns?

_____

_____

b   What are chocolate truffles?

_____

_____

c   What is veal?

_____

_____

d   What are pommes de terre lyonnaises?

_____

_____

e   What is custard?

_____

_____

f What is a soufflé?

_____

_____

g What is salmon?

_____

_____

h What is a leek?

_____

_____

2 Now think of three dishes that are popular in your country but that foreign visitors might not know. Write short explanations of what they are.

a _____

_____

b _____

_____

c _____

_____

Exercise 5

You are working at the reception desk of a busy hotel. Using your own ideas, offer help to the guests. Use **will** in your answers.

Example:
'The TV in my room doesn't seem to be working properly.'
I'll send someone up to fix it straight away.

a 'I'm afraid I haven't got any cash on me to pay for this guidebook.'

_____

b 'I'm afraid I've bent my room key and it doesn't open the door.'

_____

c 'I need to get into town as soon as possible.'

_____

d 'Would it be possible for you to look after my passport and traveller's cheques?'

_____

e 'I need to phone Mr Jamieson at the Imperial Hotel, but I haven't got the phone number.'

_____

Exercise 6   Fill the gaps in these two dialogues with **will** or **going to** and the verb in brackets. The first one has been done for you.

GUEST 1: Could you let me have £5? I ¹*am going to buy* (buy) a few things from the gift shop.

GUEST 2: Of course. What ²_____ (you/buy)?

GUEST 1: I ³_____ (get) some postcards.

GUEST 2: Do they sell papers as well?

GUEST 1: I ⁴_____ (have) a look for you.

    I ⁵_____ (get) you *The Times* if they have one.

GUEST: Could you ring Mr Hazlett in Room 527 for me?

RECEPTION: Certainly, I ⁶_____ (ring) him now . . . I'm afraid there's no reply, but I ⁷_____ (give) him a message if you like.

GUEST: Thanks. Could you tell him that I've got some theatre tickets, and that we ⁸_____ (see) 'Hamlet'?

RECEPTION: OK. I ⁹_____ (let) him know.

Exercise 7   Make sentences from the jumbled words, and use them to complete the dialogue in the restaurant. One has been done for you.

a the in like you table would corner
I'll right one get away
done steaks like you would how your
wine the menu here and is the list
some meal like order you with wine to would your
a for table like you would two
you to now are ready order
to like follow what would you
as you like would what a starter
you like order would aperitif to an

WAITER: Good evening, sir. ¹*Would you like a table for two?*

GUEST: Yes, please.

WAITER: ²_____

GUEST: Yes, that would be fine. It looks nice and quiet over there.

WAITER: ³_____

GUEST: Yes, please, a Cinzano and a dry Martini.

WAITER: Certainly, sir. ⁴_____

GUEST: Thank you.

WAITER: ⁵_____

GUEST: Yes, we are.

WAITER: ⁶_____

GUEST: The snails and one mixed salad, please.

WAITER: ⁷_____

GUEST: Two fillet steaks with maître d'hôtel butter, please.

WAITER: Certainly. ⁸_____

GUEST: One medium rare, and the other well done.

WAITER: ⁹_____

GUEST: Yes, please. A bottle of Rioja.

WAITER: ¹⁰_____

Exercise 8

You are working as a receptionist. Two guests speak to you. Write down the messages you would take for the Concierge, and Mr Harvey. Try to make the messages as short but as clear as you can. The first one has been started for you.

1 'I've been trying to get hold of the concierge, but she doesn't seem to be in. Anyway, it's about the excursion you're doing to the Acropolis tomorrow. What we really need to know is what happens and how much it all costs, and then we can make up our minds about whether or not to go. So could you ask her to give us a ring? It's Mr Hertz and we're in Room 284. Thanks.'

CONCIERGE: Mr Hertz (284) _____

_____

_____

_____

_____

_____

2 'Could I have a word with John Harvey? He's in Room 635. Oh, he's out, is he? Could you let him know I rang and I'll call back later – the name's Peter Franks.'

_____

_____

_____

_____

_____

_____

Unit 6

Exercise 1

Complete the dialogue by choosing the best option from the words in italics. The first one has been done for you.

GUEST: I'd like to ¹<u>check out</u>/depart now, please.

HOTEL: Certainly, madam. May I ²have/know your room number?

GUEST: Yes, it's 429 and the name's Ann Smith.

HOTEL: ³I'll/I'm going to get your bill straight ⁴up/away.

GUEST: Thank you.

HOTEL: ⁵Here/Here you are, madam. Would you like to ⁶verify/check it?

GUEST: Thank you. ⁷There's/I have just one thing – do you know what these extras are ⁸from/for?

HOTEL: Phone calls, I think, but ⁹I'll/I'm going to check, if you like.

GUEST: No, don't ¹⁰mind/worry, that ¹¹can/must be right. Everything ¹²appears/seems fine.

HOTEL: How ¹³would/will you like to ¹⁴pay/buy?

GUEST: You ¹⁵accept/receive Visa, ¹⁶isn't it/don't you?

HOTEL: Yes, ¹⁷we do/it is.

GUEST: Here you are.

Exercise 2

1 Match the calculations in column A with the answers in column B. They all relate to prices at a New York hotel. The first one has been done for you.

A		B	
1 <u>b</u>	$45 + 10%	a	is $2.70.
2 __	$200 − 15%	b	comes to $49.50.
3 __	£100 at $1.624 to the £	c	comes to $3 each.
4 __	$12 ÷ 4	d	is $170.
5 __	$121.25 × 4	e	comes to $162.40.
6 __	$0.90 × 3	f	is $485.

2 Now decide which calculation above is relevant. Write out the calculation as you would say it.

Example:
Lunch for two in the hotel restaurant including the service charge.
Forty-five dollars plus ten per cent comes to forty-nine dollars and fifty cents.

a The price of a standard room from Monday to Friday lunchtime.

_____

b The cost of three Coca-Colas from the mini-bar.

_____

c   The amount in dollars you would receive when changing £100 at the bureau de change.

_____

d   The price of an executive room with a corporate discount.

_____

e   The cost per person of a ten-minute taxi ride shared by four people.

_____

Exercise 3

Answer the clues to find the hidden word. The first one has been done for you.

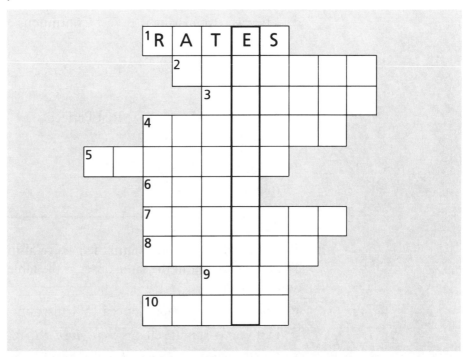

1 Room ___ for our regular corporate guests are lower than those for individual bookings. (5)
2 In a Visa transaction, give the guest the top copy of the ___ . (7)
3 I'd like to pay by ___ card. Do you accept American Express? (6)
4 No, there's no need to pay a ___ . You can just leave us your passport as security. (7)
5 If you go on a package tour, you may have to pay in ___ . (7)
6 I haven't got any ___ on me – could you lend me 50p for the bus? (4)
7 If you have still got the ___ , the shop will give you a refund. (7)
8 I've got my guarantee card, but I can't seem to find my ___ book. (6)
9 Could you prepare my bill, please? I'd like to check ___ now. (3)
10 I've got £50 – could you give me ten £5 ___ ? (5)

Exercise 4   1   Fill the gaps in this table with the correct form of the verb **be**. The first
one has been done for you.

ACTIVE	TENSE	PASSIVE
a They inspect the rooms every day.	Present Simple	The rooms *are* inspected every day.
b They're cleaning your room now.	Present Continuous	Your room _____ _____ cleaned now.
c They sent the bill to the company.	Simple Past	The bill _____ sent to the company.
d They were preparing the bill.	Past Continuous	The bill _____ _____ prepared.
e They have redecorated the bar.	Present Perfect	The bar _____ _____ redecorated.
f They had made a mistake.	Past Perfect	A mistake _____ _____ made.
g They will do it tomorrow.	Future	It _____ done tomorrow.

2   Transform these sentences into the passive, using the seven tenses above.
The tenses are not in the same order as the table. The first one has been
done for you.

a   They gave corporate clients a 15% discount last year.

Last year corporate clients *were given a 15% discount.*

b   I'm afraid they are emptying the pool for maintenance.

I'm afraid the pool _____

c   We ask guests to check out by 12.00.

Guests _____

d   We will return guests' laundry by 9 a.m. the following morning.

Guests' laundry _____

e   I didn't know if the bill had included service.

I didn't know if service _____

f   Why hasn't anyone paid this bill yet?

Why _____

g   He called a taxi while they were bringing down his luggage.

He called a taxi while his _____

Exercise 5

Arrange the sentences below into two passages. They both describe the procedures to follow when accepting credit cards; the first passage is a formal description issued by the credit card company, and in the second passage a hotel employee is telling a new trainee informally what to do. One sentence from each passage has been given.

a   If the date is still valid, an authorization code should be obtained from the credit card company.

b   Then you fill in the voucher and ask them to sign it while you are looking.

c   When they've signed it, check that the signatures are the same.

d   First of all, make sure that the card isn't out of date.

e   If they are, you give them back their card and the top sheet of the voucher, and that's it.

f   In order to prevent credit card fraud, the following procedures must be followed.

g   Firstly, the expiry date of the card must be checked.

h   Finally, if the signatures match, the card and the top copy of the voucher should be returned to the customer.

i   If it's still valid, you phone the credit card company for an authorization number.

j   Basically, what you have to do is this.

k   The voucher should be filled in and signed in the presence of the employee.

l   The signatures on the card and voucher should be compared.

Formal description

1 *In order to prevent credit card fraud, the following procedures must be followed.*

2 _____

3 _____

4 _____

5 _____

6 _____

Informal instructions

1 *Basically, what you have to do is this.*

2 _____

3 _____

4 _____

5 _____

6 _____

Exercise 6   The manager of the Bear Island Hotel has received this letter. Read the information and the brochure and choose a suitable suite for Mr and Mrs Hayward.

We would like to come for a total of five nights from February 10th. This time we would prefer a small suite with a double bed, balcony, and, if possible, a view of the sea.

I would be grateful if you could send me details of prices and availability, and look forward to hearing from you.

SUITE	ACCOMMODATION	MINIMUM NUMBER OF GUESTS	PRICE PER PERSON PER NIGHT★
DOVE	Twin-bedded room, separate sitting-room, private bathroom, sea views	1	£45
(Single person supplement £15 per night)			
WYE	Double bedroom, separate sitting-room, private bathroom, sea views	2	£48
DERWENT	Double bedroom, separate sitting-room, private bathroom, sea views, balcony	2	£50
LATHKILL (When occupied by three persons, a supplement of £15 per night is payable.)	Two double bedrooms, separate sitting-room, private bathroom, sea views, balcony	3	£61

★ including full English breakfast, dinner and VAT 17.5%

SPECIAL RATES

Low season discount:
Between January 10 and April 22, bookings attract a low-season discount of 10%.

Long stay discounts:
Bookings for five nights or more attract a further discount of 10%.

Now complete the reply and reservation form.

Bear Island Hotel
Porthleven, Cornwall

Mr M Hayward   16 November 19__
10 Hollybush Lane
Elsfield OXON OX2 3AU

Dear Mr Hayward

Thank you very much for your enquiry regarding a possible reservation for a
suite for yourself and your wife for [1]_____ nights from [2]_____ .
   We can offer the [3]_____ Suite, which has a separate sitting-room and
a private bathroom, and also has a [4]_____ with wonderful sea views.
The standard rate for the Suite is [5]_____ per person per night, which
includes a full [6]_____ and [7]_____ and tax. However, as you will be
coming in [8]_____ , we would be able to offer you a discount of
[9]_____ .In addition, we offer a further discount of [10]_____ for
stays of [11]_____ nights or more. The total would therefore be
[12]_____ including VAT.
   Should you decide to visit us, I would be grateful if you could return
the enclosed booking form.

I look forward to hearing from you.

Yours sincerely

Jennifer Howard

Jennifer Howard
Reservations Manager

RESERVATION FORM

Name [1]_____

Address [2]_____

_____ Postcode [3]_____ Telephone No.[4]_____

Please reserve accomodation for [5]_____ person/people in the [6]_____ Suite for

[7]_____ nights arriving on [8]_____ and departing on [9]_____

I enclose my cheque to the value of [10]£ _____ being one quarter of the total cost of my stay.
I understand that this deposit may be forfeited in the event of cancellation or curtailment.

Signature [11]_____ Date [12]_____

Unit 7

Exercise 1

First of all, read paragraph 1. Then choose one of the options, A, B, or C. The option will tell you which paragraph to read next. For example, if you choose option C after paragraph 1, it says 'GO TO 18'. This means you must go to paragraph 18 and continue reading there. The aim is to find the best solution to the problem.

1 A guest at your hotel comes up to you and says, 'I have a complaint to make. The room I'm in is terribly noisy.' Should you . . .
A offer to change the guest's room?   GO TO 19.
B ask the guest to tell you more about the noise?   GO TO 9.
C say that there are no other rooms available?   GO TO 18.

2 The manager calls you into his office. He has heard about what happened and says that you have handled the situation very badly. He explains that the hotel is already overstaffed, and that he is dismissing you because you have lost the hotel one of its most valuable clients. This is the end, but it is the worst solution. Go back to the beginning and try again.

3 The manager calls you into his office. He is impressed by the way you handled the situation and has decided to promote you and to give you a pay rise. This is the best solution, and the end.

4 The guest insists on seeing the manager. Do you . . .
A ask the guest to have a complimentary coffee while you sort the problem out?   GO TO 8.
B go and see the manager?   GO TO 11.
C tell the guest not to be such a nuisance?   GO TO 5.

5 The guest storms out and writes a complaint to the manager and to the local tourist board.   GO TO 2.

6 The manager hears what you have done. He says you did not handle the situation particularly well, and that in future you should do things differently.   GO TO 16.

7 You discover that the guest making the complaint is a very important customer who sends a large number of clients to the hotel. You also discover that the noisy guests are leaving today and will be replaced by a retired couple. When he returns, do you . . .
  A offer to give him a different room?   GO TO 19.
  B explain the situation, apologize, and offer him a free dinner as compensation?   GO TO 14.
  C say that he will just have to stay where he is?   GO TO 5.

8 You think about the situation and decide that the guest has a reasonable complaint. When he returns, you tell him that . . .
  A he must pay the extra, but can have a discount the next time he comes.   GO TO 5.
  B he can have the room at the original price.   GO TO 6.
  C he can have the room for the original price less 10% for the inconvenience he has suffered.   GO TO 15.

9 The guest explains that the people in the room next door had a tape recorder and were playing very loud music into the early hours of the morning. He complained but was ignored. Do you . . .
  A offer to give him a different room?   GO TO 19.
  B ask him to have a complimentary coffee while you look at the situation?   GO TO 17.
  C tell him that you will speak to the people in the next room?   GO TO 13.

10 The manager is not there.   GO BACK TO 18.

11 The manager is out.   GO BACK TO 4.

12 The manager is out.   GO BACK TO 17.

13 You cannot contact the people in the next room, so you decide to upgrade him.   GO TO 19.

14 The guest thanks you for your offer and when he leaves, he writes a note to the manager explaining how well you handled the situation.   GO TO 3.

15 The manager calls you into his office. He is not impressed by the way you handled the situation as you lost the hotel a considerable amount of money. As a result he will deduct the money from your salary to teach you a lesson.   GO TO 16.

16   The manager gives you some training material to read. It is about a guest who complains that his room is too noisy.   GO BACK TO 1 AND TRY AGAIN.

17   While he is away, you . . .
   A   deal with some important paperwork; you hope he won't come back again, but he does.   GO TO 18.
   B   check the guest profile on the computer.   GO TO 7.
   C   go and see the manager.   GO TO 12.

18   The guest is not satisfied and feels that something can be done. Do you . . .
   A   go and see the manager?   GO TO 10.
   B   upgrade him to a different room?   GO TO 19.
   C   ask him to tell you a little more about the problem?   GO TO 9.

19   The guest is happy and you allocate one of the most expensive rooms. Three days later the guest checks out, and is horrified at the size of the bill, which is more than double what he had been expecting. Do you . . .
   A   explain that the price was clearly posted on the door and that he must pay?   GO TO 4.
   B   ask the guest to have a complimentary coffee while you sort the problem out?   GO TO 8.
   C   say that he can have the room for the original price?   GO TO 6.

   What is the quickest way to the best solution? Write down the steps here:
   1B → _____
   What is the quickest way to losing your job? Write down the steps here:
   1C → _____

Exercise 2

After inspecting the rooms at 10.00 a.m., the housekeeper in a large hotel made a list of jobs that needed to be done. It is now 11.50 a.m. Write sentences about what has been done and what hasn't been done.

Example:
201 – fix lock on bathroom door.   (No)
The lock on the bathroom door in 201 hasn't been fixed.
208 – collect laundry.   (Yes)
The laundry has been collected from 208.

a   213 – mend plug.   (Yes)

_____

b   215 – replace kettle.   (No)

_____

c 316 – clean up red wine stain on carpet. (No)

_____

d 302 – change bedcovers. (Yes)

_____

e Third floor – empty bins in corridor. (Yes)

_____

f 403 – repair leaking tap. (No)

_____

g 416 – put in cot. (No)

_____

h 500 – air-conditioning needs adjusting. (Yes)

_____

Exercise 3

Read the following situations. Make two sentences about each one, using **should have** and **shouldn't have**.

Example:
Karl lost his job as a reservations clerk. He kept forgetting to write people's names in the reservations book.
He shouldn't have been so inefficient.
He should have written down the information straight away.

The receptionist at a big hotel shouted at one of the guests who pointed out that there was a mistake on his bill.

a _____
b _____

A waiter in a restaurant didn't get any tips all evening.

c _____
d _____

A chef had to throw away a steak that one of the diners sent back.

e _____
f _____

Maria got a very bad reference from her previous employer.

g _____
h _____

Henry lost someone's passport.

i _____
j _____

Exercise 4   Choose the best word to complete the sentences. Use a dictionary if you need to. The first one has been done for you.

a   Send someone up to my room at once – the bathroom hasn't been cleaned and it's *absolutely* disgusting.

   A very   **B** extremely   **C** terribly   **D** absolutely

b   The food isn't bad but the service is _____ slow.

   A absolutely   **B** utterly   **C** totally   **D** very

c   The training that they give their staff is extremely _____ .

   A brilliant   **B** magnificent   **C** good   **D** wonderful

d   The problem with holidays in England is that the weather is often very

   _____ .

   A awful   **B** terrible   **C** dreadful   **D** bad

e   This is the worst bottle of wine I have ever had. It is absolutely

   _____ – it tastes like vinegar.

   A bad   **B** sour   **C** disgusting   **D** unpleasant

f   I'm _____ sorry Room Service haven't brought you your coffee yet. I'll ask them to bring it up straight away.

   A bitterly   **B** quite   **C** absolutely   **D** terribly

g   Please tell the chef that was the best steak I have ever had. It was

   _____ marvellous.

   A terribly   **B** absolutely   **C** very   **D** extremely

h   The room I'm in is _____ small. I must insist on having another one.

   A quite   **B** absolutely   **C** totally   **D** extremely

i   I'm certainly not going in the pool – it looks very _____ .

   A dirty   **B** filthy   **C** disgusting   **D** revolting

j   The last hotel where I worked was absolutely _____ – there were over 900 bedrooms.

   A enormous   **B** big   **C** large   **D** high

Exercise 5 Using the words and phrases below, complete this letter of apology. It is from the manager of the Frankfurt Palace to a guest who complained that the restaurant did not cater for his request for *halal* food. (*Halal* food is eaten by Muslims and has to be prepared in a special way.) The first one has been done for you.

adequate notice
As a sign of our concern
I can assure you
I hope
in advance
I was sorry to hear

I would like to point out
Please accept
sincerely
Thank you for
Unfortunately

Dear Dr Abdulrahman,

[1]*Thank you for* your letter of 18 May.

[2]_____ that you were unable to obtain *halal* food from the restaurant and that you had to eat out for the night that you spent with us. You are quite right to say that the brochure states that we cater for our guests' special diets. However, [3]_____ that the brochure also makes it clear that we require [4]_____ because we need to make special arrangements.

[5]_____ we were not informed of your requirements [6]_____ and so were unable to meet them. [7]_____, however, that we will be able to provide *halal* food when you next come to stay with us if you can give us three days' notice.

[8]_____, I would like to offer you a $25 voucher towards the cost of your next visit, and [9]_____ we will have the pleasure of your custom again.

[10]_____ my apologies for the inconvenience you suffered.

Yours [11]_____

BG Lagerfeld

B G Lagerfeld
Manager

Unit 8

Exercise 1

Read the Information Sheets which describe some of the activities available at the Sherwood Holiday Village, and answer these questions. The first one has been started for you.

a Which activities offer tuition?

Archery, fencing, _____

b Which activities are not available on Mondays?

_____

c Which activities take place outside the grounds of Sherwood?

_____

d What would be the price for a Parent and Child Musketeer fencing session of an hour and fifteen minutes?

_____

e What activities are available for a child aged six?

_____

f Which activities require special clothing of some kind?

_____

g How much would two hours' windsurfing (without tuition) cost if you brought all your own equipment?

_____

h Which activity could be done late in the evening?

_____

i Which is the most expensive activity?

_____

ARCHERY

LOCATION	At a local venue.
	Transport is provided from Reception.
TIMES	Monday: 10.30 a.m.
	Tuesday - Thursday: 9.30 a.m., 12 noon, 2.30 p.m.
	Sunday: 10.30 a.m.
SESSION	45 minutes.
EQUIPMENT	All provided.
TUITION	Available, with current European Champion.
MINIMUM AGE	10 years.
TARIFF	£4.70 per person per session.

CLAY PIGEON SHOOTING

LOCATION	At a local ground. Transport is provided from the main reception.
TIMES	Daily except Monday and Friday.
SESSION	1 hour.
EQUIPMENT	All provided. Guns, including lightweight and ladies', cartridges, clays, hearing protection.
TUITION	Full tuition given.
EXPERIENCE	Not necessary.
MINIMUM AGE	15 years.
TARIFF	£6.50 per person per session.

FENCING

LOCATION	Country Club Aerobics Studio.
TIMES	Wednesday and Saturday (September onwards).
SESSION	1 hour 15 minutes.
	Designed for those new to the sport.
	Special activity for younger children: Parent and Child Musketeer, where only the adults are hit.
	Sabre fencing for those who have fenced before. Follow-on sessions for those wishing to improve.
EQUIPMENT	All provided. Long trousers should be worn.
TUITION	Full tuition is given.
	British Academy of Fencing Professional Coach.
MINIMUM AGE	9 years (6 years for Parent and Child Musketeer).
TARIFF	Adult £5.75 Child £3.85

HORSE RIDING

LOCATION	At a local stables. Transport provided from Reception. Allow approximately 1 hour and 30 mins.
TIMES	Daily as demand dictates.
NOVICES	Slow pony trek. Walking only. Maximum of 10 people. Mimimum age 7 years, maximum weight 16 stones.
	Beginners, riding lessons - daily 4.15 p.m. except Monday. Minimum age 5 years. Lessons at other times by arrangement.
INTERMEDIATE	Trekking, walking and trotting. Mimimum age 7 years, maximum weight 16 stones. Riding lessons by arrangement.
ADVANCED	Hack, walking and trotting. Minimum age 7 years, maximum weight 15 stones. Riding lessons such as dressage and showjumping by arrangement.
EQUIPMENT	Hard hats provided. Trousers, flat shoes or boots with small heel must be worn.
TARIFF	Beginner lessons £9.80. Intermediate and advanced lessons £12.00.
	Slow pony trek £9.80
	Intermediate trek £12.50
	Fast trek (hack) £14.30

TEN-PIN BOWLING

LOCATION	Leisure Bowl.
TIMES	8.00 a.m. - 11.45 p.m.
SESSION	45 minutes.
EQUIPMENT	All provided, including shoes
TOURNAMENT	Please see the Bowling Coach if you wish to take part in Sherwood Ten-Pin Bowling Tournament.
TARIFF	£8.35 per lane per 45 mins.
	Please note that Ten-Pin Bowling is a very popular sport and we advise you to book early to avoid disappointment.

WINDSURFING

EQUIPMENT	We have 3.65m and 3.25m boards available. A full range of sails is available for 7-year-olds to adults. Wetsuits and wetsuit boots are available for hire and it is recommended that these are worn.
PRIVATE BOARDS	A launch fee is charged. Please ensure you have adequate third party insurance.
SAFETY	Buoyancy aids must be worn. Sherwood wetsuit boots must be worn. Wetsuits are recommended and may be hired. Tuition is strongly advised for novices.
RYA COURSES	We offer nationally recognized courses. Ask at the Watersports' Kiosk for details.
TARIFF	per hour £3.50 per two hours £5.60
	Tuition - 1 person per hour £17.00 2 persons per hour £26.50 3 persons per hour £37.00
	Launch of private board £3.00 per day

Exercise 2   A hotel guest is making enquiries about a guided tour on behalf of his young daughter. Fill in the blanks with the correct form of the verb. The first one has been done for you.

GUEST: Could you give me a little more information about your City Tours tomorrow? My daughter would like to see the sights, but we'll be leaving for the airport at about five, so if she ¹*decides* (decide) to go on a tour, she ²_____ (must) be back by 4.30.

CONCIERGE: Right, well, there are three tours tomorrow, so I'll just check the times for you. First of all there's the Acropolis Tour, and if she ³_____ (go) on that one, she ⁴_____ (get back) here at four, so that would be all right. If she ⁵_____ (choose) the Corinth Canal Tour, she ⁶_____ (not/return) until the evening, so that's not suitable. The other one is the tour of the museum, and there are two visits – one in the morning and one in the afternoon.

GUEST: What time ⁷_____ (she/get back) if she ⁸_____ (go) on the early morning visit?

CONCIERGE: If there ⁹_____ (be) a slight delay because of traffic or something, it still means that she ¹⁰_____ (have) plenty of time.

GUEST: OK, well, I'll think about it, and if she ¹¹_____ (decide) to do that, I ¹²_____ (let you know).

CONCIERGE: That's fine, but please ¹³_____ (make) a reservation if she ¹⁴_____ (want) to go, because they do get booked up quickly, and there's a chance that she ¹⁵_____ (not/get) a place if you ¹⁶_____ (not/book) early.

Exercise 3   Use your own ideas, based on the following notes, to write First Conditional sentences beginning with **If**.

Example:
A driving licence is necessary to hire a car.
If you haven't got a driving licence, you can't hire a car.

a   Breakfast can be ordered by ringing room service.

_____

b We offer 10% discount for cash payments.

_____

c TOTAL SUN BLOCK CREAM – protection factor 30.

_____

d Disco – minimum age, sixteen.

_____

e Cheques are welcome when supported by a valid guarantee card.

_____

f Courtesy coach – transfer time to airport, thirty-five minutes.

_____

g Early booking for the Santorini Tour is essential.

_____

h Guests are advised not to leave valuables in their rooms.

_____

Exercise 4

Imagine you are working in a hotel in your home town. A number of guests ask you for your advice and suggestions. Use your own ideas to make three different suggestions in each situation.

Example:
'I've got the whole morning free. Is there anything interesting I could do?'

a *Why don't you have a look at the local museum?*
b *If I were you, I'd spend the morning in the covered market.*
c *You could always visit some of the colleges.*

1 'I'd like to look round town, but I don't want to hire a car.'

a _____
b _____
c _____

2 'I'd like to take back a small present for my wife. Any ideas?'

a _____
b _____
c _____

3 'I don't feel like staying in tonight. What sort of things are on in town?'

a _____
b _____
c _____

Exercise 5

Read the description of a tour organized by a hotel in Nepal. Number the different methods of transport shown in the pictures in the order in which they are used on the tour. The first one has been done for you.

RIVER & JUNGLE TOUR

Kathmandu-Rafting-Chitwan-Kathmandu
5 DAYS

Day 1 Drive by air-conditioned coach to the put-in point on the Trishuli River at the small village of Kuringhat. The day is spent rafting in a long forested canyon which offers a number of challenging rapids. Overnight camp on a sandy beach.

Day 2 A more leisurely pace, we float by the towns of Devghat and Narayanghat. Camp at the confluence point of the Kali Gandaki and Trishuli Rivers.

Day 3 Enter the Royal Chitwan National Park and float down to the Tharu Village. Here you have an excellent chance to see a wealth of waterfowl and some large mammals on the riverbanks. From Amaltarighat, travel in style by bullock cart to the Tiger Tops Tharu Village. Afternoon venture on ponyback to observe life in nearby Tharu hamlets or relax by the pool. Enjoy a cultural programme before dinner.

Day 4 A boat trip across the Naranyi River and a Landrover drive with sightseeing en route brings you to the Tiger Tops Tented Camp. Enjoy an elephant safari and a jungle walk accompanied by naturalists. Overnight at the Camp.

Day 5 Enjoy an early-morning nature walk in the densely forested Surung Valley before driving to Meghauli airstrip for the short flight to Kathmandu. Transfer to your hotel.

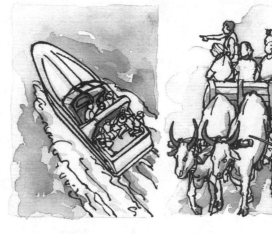

a   b

c *1*   d

e   f   g   h

Exercise 6   Answer the clues to find the hidden word. All the words are connected with renting cars.

1 The price includes collision damage ___ , so you don't have to pay if you have an accident. (6)
2 In certain countries, we can offer one-way ___ , so you can pick up the car in one city and leave it in another. (6)
3 In the US, child safety ___ are mandatory for all children under six years. (5)
4 Do you know whether this car is automatic or ___ ? (6)
5 The price quoted includes insurance for third ___ , fire and theft. (5)
6 Local government ___ are usually between 5% and 10% of the cost of hiring the car. (5)
7 When you collect the car, we will provide you with a full ___ of petrol. (4)
8 You don't need an international driving ___ – a British one is fine. (7)
9 The price includes unlimited ___ , so you can drive as much as you like with no extra charge. (7)

Unit 9

Exercise 1

A company in London has invited a group of important clients from Japan for a series of meetings. Look at the information about the two hotels they are considering for the group, and complete the sentences with **like**, **unlike**, **just as**, and **whereas**.

	PALACE	REGATTA
Secretarial services	Yes	Yes
Experience of dealing with Japanese clients	Yes	Yes
Member of staff who speaks Japanese	Yes	Yes
Japanese food in the restaurant	No	Yes
Signs and information in Japanese	No	Yes
Translating facilities	Yes	Yes
Special services for business guests	Yes	Yes
Generous discounts	No	Yes
Conference room	1 only	Choice of 6

Example:
Like the Palace, the Regatta provides a range of secretarial services.

a _____ the Palace, the Regatta has experience of dealing with Japanese clients.

b _____ the Palace employs someone who speaks Japanese, the Regatta also has a member of staff who speaks it.

c _____ the Palace, the Regatta has a restaurant that serves a wide range of Japanese food.

d The Palace only has signs and information in English, _____ the Regatta has signs and information in Japanese as well.

e The Palace offers translating facilities, _____ the Regatta does.

f _____ the Palace, the Regatta provides special services for business guests.

g The Palace does not offer any discounts, _____ the Regatta's discounts are very generous.

h _____ the Palace, the Regatta has a good choice of conference rooms.

Exercise 2

Write questions beginning **How long** in response to these statements. Use the Present Perfect Continuous of the verbs in brackets.

Example:
'I'm getting more confident about speaking Japanese.' (you/learn it)
How long have you been learning it?

a 'I know my way around London much better now.'   (you/live there)

_____

b 'This hotel feels like a second home.'   (you/stay here)

_____

c 'I work for Thomsons, the tour operators.'   (you/work for them)

_____

d 'You're back at last! Mrs Schmidt is in your office.'   (she/wait for me)

_____

e 'They give us a good discount here because we're regular
   customers.'   (you/come here)

_____

f 'As you can see, we've got a very good range of conference
   facilities.'   (you/have conferences here)

_____

Exercise 3   Reply to the following questions and statements using the words in
                    brackets and the Present Perfect Continuous with **for** or **since**.

                    Example:
                    'How long have you had the new chef?'   (He/work here/three months)
                    He's been working here for three months.

a 'Is this your first trip to Athens?'   (No/I/come here/years)

_____

b 'Are you new here?'   (No/I/work here/last September)

_____

c 'You speak very good English.'   (Thank you/I/study it/five years)

_____

d 'Is this the first group from Korea that you've looked after?'   (No/we/
   look after them/a long time)

_____

e 'The Concierge doesn't seem very competent.'   (He/not/do the job/
   very long)

_____

f 'You have a wonderful herb garden here.'   (We/grow/all our own
   herbs/the hotel opened)

_____

Exercise 4

In the following dialogues, put the verbs in brackets into the Present Perfect Simple or the Present Perfect Continuous. The first one has been done for you as an example.

GUEST: Hello. Is there something wrong with Room Service? I ¹*have been waiting* (wait) for my breakfast for over twenty minutes, and it still isn't here.

RECEPTION: I'm sorry, sir. I'll give them a ring. May I have your room number?

GUEST: 328. In fact, I ²_____ (ring) them three times but they're always engaged.

RECEPTION: I do apologize. I'll go round to them personally and see what's going on.

GUEST 1: Is this the first time your company ³_____ (use) this hotel?

GUEST 2: No, we ⁴_____ (have) two or three conferences here, and we like it. What about you?

GUEST 1: We're very old customers here. We ⁵_____ (come) here for the last twenty years.

MANAGER: How are you getting on with this morning's post?

SECRETARY: I ⁶_____ (deal) with most of it. We ⁷_____ (have) two bookings for July, and I ⁸_____ (pay) all of the bills. I ⁹_____ (write) to Carson Ltd to ask if they want any special arrangements for their manager who's coming next week. Oh, one other thing, we'd better get someone to look at the fax machine – someone ¹⁰_____ (try) to get through since about nine this morning, but the machine doesn't seem to be working properly.

Exercise 5

1 On the next page is a magazine report about a new Hyatt hotel in Spain. Put the paragraphs into the correct order. The first one has been done for you.

a ___ Hyatt's latest venture is the Hyatt La Manga Club, a 1400-acre resort on the southern coast of Spain. Hyatt has totally redeveloped this resort, with three 18-hole championship golf courses, seventeen tennis courts and a variety of watersports.

b ___ The majority of those playing golf on business, however, stressed that making contacts and winning new business was an integral part of their rationale for spending so much time on the fairways and putting greens.

c _1_ Golf, hotels, and business travellers have long been a well-established combination, so it was no surprise that Hyatt came up with the idea of carrying out a survey of the business golfer's attitude to the game.

d ___ A central part of the resort is the recently opened Hotel Principe Felipe, a 192-room hotel designed in the Andalusian style of the region and overlooking the golf courses. Hyatt hopes the new complex will meet the needs of a wide range of business travellers and other golfing enthusiasts.

e ___ In addition to the most recent survey, other research carried out by Hyatt had shown that a quarter of the 30 million golfers in the US were top management executives. It therefore developed a strategy of developing hotel resort complexes, complete with golf courses and other health facilities.

f ___ Hyatt interviewed over 400 golfing executives and found that the way they played was very similar to their behaviour in the boardroom: more than a third, for example, admitted cheating on the golf course as well as cheating at work. Highly-motivated achievers also preferred playing long, hilly courses to anything that was too easy for their skills.

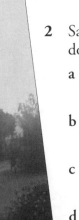

2 Say if the following statements are true or false. The first one has been done for you.

a Hyatt conducted its recent survey to see how they could get more executives to play golf. *False*

b Most of the executives that Hyatt interviewed said they cheated at golf. _____

c Highly motivated executives did not like short, simple golf courses. _____

d Most of the people they interviewed said they played golf to make contacts. _____

e An early Hyatt survey in the US showed that there were about 7.5 million top management executives who played golf. _____

f Hyatt decided to develop the La Manga resort after interviewing 400 golfing executives. _____

g Hyatt's resort in La Manga offers a range of other sporting activities besides golf. _____

h The style of the hotel reflects the architecture in the local area. _____

Exercise 6

You work at the Country Park Hotel. You have been asked to complete this letter which will be mailed to your existing business customers. In paragraph 1, describe the suites in the new Business Wing of the hotel which has just been completed; in paragraph 2, remind them of the other facilities that the hotel has. Look at the photographs for ideas.

Dear Guest

We are pleased to announce that we have recently completed a Business Wing which has been designed to meet the needs of business travellers.

1 In the Business Wing, you will find everything that a busy executive needs.

_____

_____

_____

_____

_____

2 In addition to this, we also offer a wide range of other facilities and sporting activities.

_____

_____

_____

_____

_____

We look forward to welcoming you to the Country Park again.

Yours faithfully

Jenny Parson, Promotions Executive

Exercise 7   Answer the clues to find the hidden word. The first one has been done for you.

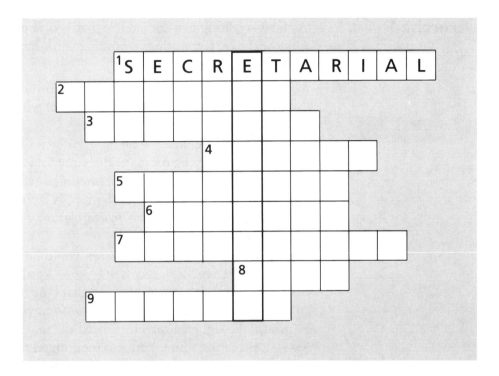

1 As part of the service we offer our business guests, we provide a range of ___ services including typing, photocopying, and filing. (11)
2 The TVs in the business suites are all equipped with ___ so you can check on the latest news or stock market figures. (8)
3 Could you let me have an ___ projector so that the people in the meeting can see the charts I'm referring to? (8)
4 When you're using the projector, you can pull down the ___ from the ceiling rather than use the wall. (6)
5 Each Business Suite has the latest IBM-compatible personal ___ loaded with software. (8)
6 In each Business Suite there is a bedroom and a separate ___ room for up to eight people. (7)
7 Rooms are provided with a full range of ___ including writing paper, envelopes, and paper for the fax. (10)
8 We treat all our guests well, but we take special care with people like top company directors, who are classified as ___ . (4)
9 Could you let me have a new cartridge for the ___ , please? It seems to have run out of ink. (7)

Unit 10

Exercise 1

A client is talking to a conference manager about his requirements. Choose the correct options from the words in italics. The first one has been done for you.

MANAGER: Could we just [1]*run/see/speak* through your [2]*wants/wishes/requirements*, and I'll give you an idea of what rooms would be [3]*fine/well/suitable*.

CLIENT: Yes, of course. We'll be starting at six in the evening, and we'll need three meeting rooms at the same time. The Chief Executive Officer will be [4]*giving/saying/addressing* a talk to the sales force, so we'll need a room for about a hundred or so [5]*members/audience/delegates*.

MANAGER: What sort of [6]*chair/seating/sitting* arrangements will you need for that?

CLIENT: Theatre-[7]*method/style/way* would be fine for that, because it's not a [8]*workroom/workshop/workhouse*. We also need another room for the technical support group, and that'll be for about thirty-five people, and that'll have to be [9]*teaching/lesson/classroom*-style. And the last group, the eighteen directors, need the same.

MANAGER: That's fine. You also mentioned something about an [10]*demonstration/exhibition/manifestation*.

CLIENT: Yes, really we're looking for a fairly large room – something in the region of 200 to 250 [11]*square/squared/cubic* metres.

MANAGER: That's no problem. I can think of a couple of [12]*occasions/possibilities/chances*.

CLIENT: Good, and then afterwards we'll need a room for dinner, and we're [13]*awaiting/intending/expecting* about a hundred and sixty to a hundred and eighty for that, but I'll let you have the [14]*accurate/exact/defined* figures nearer the time.

MANAGER: That's all fine. Are there any other things that you can [15]*think of/consider/require*?

CLIENT: Oh yes, there's one other thing – the exhibition needs [16]*allowance/space/place* for a twenty-five metre stand, so we're looking for a room that's a rectangle rather than a square.

Exercise 2

Read through the information about the rooms available at the Bournemouth International Centre. Which five rooms would be suitable for the client in Exercise 1? Write the name of the room in each case. The first one has been done for you.

a The CEO's meeting with the sales staff: *the Stour Room*

b The technical support group meeting: _____

c The directors' meeting: _____

d The exhibition: _____

e The dinner: _____

BOURNEMOUTH INTERNATIONAL CENTRE
CONFERENCE FACILITIES

	Seating capacities				Area	Dimensions	
	Theatre-style	Classroom-style	Banqueting-style	Cocktail-style	Sq.m. gross	Metres	Mimimum ceiling height (mtrs)
Windsor Hall	3900	800	1200	3000	1822	40.0 x 47.0	7.0
Tregonwell Hall	1200	350	420	850	723	33.9 x 23.0	7.0
Purbeck Lounge	240	120	150	250	227	29.1 x 7.8	2.7
Purbeck Bar	70	40	60	140	171	22.5 x 7.6	2.38
Stour Room	120	70	60	100	89	7.7 x 11.5	2.46
Avon Room	55	30	35	80	48	5.7 x 8.5	2.49
President's Suite	40	20	20	60	40	4.1 x 9.8	2.45
Bourne Lounge	390	95	225	420	256	16.0 x 16.0	2.46

Exercise 3   Look at the following conference rooms. Write a short passage for a publicity brochure, following the Carlton Room example.

Carlton Room
- Size: 6m x 8m
- Uses: board meetings, presentations, workshops
- Seating capacity: 32 theatre-style, 16 boardroom-style
- Equipment: 10 power sockets, TV point, 4 telephone points
- Other: video recorder, OHP and screen

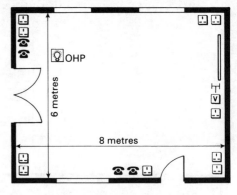

Example:

The Carlton is a rectangular room six metres wide by eight metres long and can be used for board meetings, presentations, and workshops. It has a seating capacity of 32 in theatre-style and can hold sixteen people in boardroom-style. It is equipped with ten power sockets, a TV point, four telephone points, and has also got a video recorder, and an OHP and screen.

Telford Room
- Size: 16m x 16m
- Uses: exhibitions, meetings, wedding receptions
- Seating capacity: 215 theatre-style, 220 reception-style
- Equipment: air-conditioning, PA sytem, lectern, 35mm projector and screen
- Other: large windows providing natural daylight, stage area

_____

_____

_____

_____

_____

_____

_____

_____

Tudor Hall
- Size: 43m x 46m + 8m x 5m
- Uses: major international conferences
- Seating capacity: 3900 (theatre-style only)
- Equipment: projection room, screen, simultaneous translation facilities
- Other: bar, coffee lounge, toilets

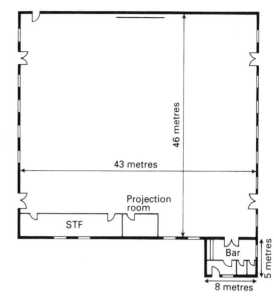

_____

_____

_____

_____

_____

_____

_____

_____

_____

Exercise 4

One of your colleagues is working in Reception during a conference. He has been asked to provide the following items, but he does not understand English very well. Explain what the items are. Use a dictionary if you need to. The first one has been done for you.

a corkscrew   a flip-chart
a lectern   a bottle opener
a transparency   an OHP marker
an Autocue   a stapler

a *A corkscrew is used for getting the cork out of a bottle.*

b _____

c _____

d _____

e _____

f _____

g _____

h _____

Exercise 5   Read this extract from a brochure. Fill in the gaps with the following words. The first one has been done for you.

advantage	but	chance
example	facilities	has
including	makes	offers
pool	acres	some
soon	provided	success
such	team	to
venue	style	whether

⊛ ⊛ ⊛ ⊛ ⊛

Set in over 100 [1]*acres* of beautiful woodland, park, and landscaped garden, Down Hall is a perfect [2]_____ of quality craftsmanship from the Victorian age. This Italian-style mansion [3]_____ recently undergone many innovative changes [4]_____ provide the very best conference facilities for today's and tomorrow's needs.

It is not just its uniqueness that [5]_____ Down Hall an excellent conference [6]_____ , but also its atmosphere of tranquillity and elegance. As [7]_____ as you enter Down Hall, you realize that it is not just a hotel, [8]_____ an experience.

Down Hall [9]_____ a selection of indoor and outdoor leisure [10]_____ to provide relaxation and a [11]_____ to unwind from a busy schedule.

A heated leisure [12]_____ , whirlpool, sauna, croquet and putting lawns are just [13]_____ of the activities offered.

Uniqueness is the keynote at Down Hall, and [14]_____ a conference is for two or 310, the same individual attention and individual service is [15]_____ by the experienced conference support [16]_____ . Down Hall has twenty-six meeting rooms, [17]_____ sixteen purpose-built syndicate rooms of exceptional proportions. Tailor-made to specific requirements, conference planners can take full [18]_____ of the expertise in providing special theme events [19]_____ as archery, laser shooting, and quad bikes.

Theatre- or classroom- [20]_____ , or informal discussion, Down Hall offers the right atmosphere guaranteed to make your event a [21]_____ .

Exercise 6

You have received an enquiry about your conference facilities. Write out the letter which will accompany the brochure that you send out. Use the following notes to help you complete the letter. The first paragraph has been started for you.

Paragraph 1
writing/introduce/Hollway House/best conference centre/London.
please/enclosed/brochure/which/explain.

Paragraph 2
Hollway House/perfect venue/conferences, training courses, etc.
provide/latest facilities/atmosphere/peaceful elegance.
proud/excellent cuisine/attentive service/we believe/best in the country.

Paragraph 3
competitive prices/many extras included in 24-hour delegate rate.
provide equipment/secretarial/mineral water/newspapers/no additional charge. excellent value for money.

Paragraph 4
pleased/make arrangements/you/visit Hollway House/view facilities.
any further information/not hesitate/contact me. look forward/hearing from you

```
Dear Client

I am writing to introduce Hollway House, the _____
_____
_____
_____
_____
_____
_____
_____
_____
_____
_____
_____
_____
_____

Yours sincerely
```

Unit 11

Exercise 1

An agent for Scandinavian Seaways is welcoming a group on a familiarization tour. Complete her speech using the following verbs in the Future Continuous. The first one has been done for you.

arrive	go on	sail	stay
board	have	set off	stop
come	leave	spend	use

'Good evening, ladies and gentlemen, and on behalf of Scandinavian Seaways, I would like to welcome you to our familiarization trip aboard the *MS Prince of Scandinavia*.

I'd just like to run through our itinerary for the next few days. We ¹*will be setting off* in a few minutes, and tonight we ²_____ across the North Sea towards Denmark. If the weather holds, we ³_____ in Esbjerg tomorrow afternoon at 13.45. The coach will take us to the Hotel Pejsegarden in Braedrup, where we ⁴_____ . This is the hotel that we ⁵_____ for all our future tours as well. There will be plenty of time to settle in, and in the evening we ⁶_____ a special dinner in the hotel's famous restaurant. At midnight there will be champagne and a firework display, followed by dancing in the disco.

We ⁷_____ the next morning in the hotel, and in the afternoon we ⁸_____ a tour of the Silkeborg Lake District. We ⁹_____ back in time for afternoon coffee, and you'll be free for the rest of the evening.

The next day the coach [10]_____ at 10.00, and
we [11]_____ on the way for lunch, before
going on to Hamburg, where we [12]_____ the
MS Hamburg for the 16.30 sailing back to Harwich.'

Exercise 2

In the following sentences put the verbs in brackets into the Future
Continuous or the Future Perfect. The first one has been done for you.

a   We can't send our clients to a half-finished hotel. Are you sure that
you *will have completed* (complete) all the building work by the
beginning of the summer?

b   I'm sorry, but I can't make the meeting on the 18th. I _____
_____ (still/go round) Greece on my inspection tour, and I
don't get back until the 21st.

c   Hello, Jenny Farmer here. I'm just ringing to ask whether you
_____ (send) someone on the fam trip we
are organizing next year.

d   I can send those two brochures off for you if you like. I _____
_____ (go) past a post-box on my way to the car, so it's no
trouble.

e   We'd better put the meeting off for a couple of days. I _____
_____ (not finish) this report by tomorrow afternoon.

f   If you don't hurry up, your plane _____
(leave) by the time you get to the airport.

g   I'm off on holiday in a few days and this time next week I _____
_____ (sit) on a lovely sunny beach in the Seychelles.

h   Could I send you the information about the hotels at the end of the
month? I _____ (not/have) time to visit
them all by next Wednesday.

i   You'd better send them a fax because they _____
_____ (make) a decision by the time a letter arrives.

j   I can give John those figures. I _____
(see) him in our weekly meeting this afternoon.

Exercise 3

You have been asked to select two hotels for two different tour operators. First read the information about the hotels on this page.

Then read the information about the tour operators on the next two pages and complete the two letters as follows: in paragraphs 1 and 4 of each letter, choose the best word from the options in italics; in paragraphs 2 and 3 of each letter, recommend two hotels and give your reasons for choosing them.

Thornbury Castle

Thornbury Castle dates back to 1511, when it was built by the Duke of Buckingham. Ten years later he was executed, and the Castle was taken over by Henry VIII. Mary Tudor lived here, and when she became queen, she returned the Castle to the Duke's family.

Today, Thornbury Castle is one of the best country house hotels in the country with an internationally-acclaimed restaurant. There are eighteen luxury bedchambers overlooking England's oldest Tudor garden. Based here, you can explore the other historic houses of the area.

No. of rooms: 18.
Tariff: double room per night from £95.
No children under 12 years unless known.

Woolley Grange

WOOLLEY GRANGE is a Jacobean stone manor house in open countryside near the fine medieval town of Bradford-on-Avon. Although completely restored, the house preserves its ancient character. The bedrooms are furnished with antiques, and downstairs there are plenty of comfortable sofas and armchairs where you can curl up with a good book.

The home of Nigel and Heather Chapman and their four children and Springer spaniel, Birdie, Woolley Grange is not just another country house hotel. Unlike many, we welcome guests of all ages and the hotel has a full-time nanny and nursery.

No. of rooms: 20.
Tariff: double room for two persons per night from £89.
Children very welcome.
Attractions include: riding, swimming, children's play area, dry skiing, hot-air balloon flights.

BLOOMSBURY

This modern hotel is situated in the heart of Bloomsbury, an area of London with a long association with Britain's greatest writers, artists, and musicians. The British Museum and Covent Garden's opera house are a few minutes' walk away and the West End theatres and London's finest art galleries are all within easy reach.

No. of rooms: 281. Suites: 3.
Tariff: from £58 per person per night (2 adults sharing). Free rooms for children when accompanied by 2 adults. Under 5s eat free.

The Imperial, Torquay

Devon's best loved resort, Torquay has excellent beaches, colourful gardens, and wide-ranging holiday amenities along with a mild climate and an air of sophistication.

Established in 1866, the Imperial is one of Britain's leading resort hotels. Overlooking Torbay, the hotel is set in five acres of delightful gardens and offers extensive amenities in the grand style.

No. of rooms: 150 (17 suites). Tariff: from £64 p.p.p.n. Family: baby-listening, baby-sitting, activity programme for children. Facilities and attractions: *Agatha Christie museum, model village, indoor and outdoor heated pools, sandy beaches nearby, tennis courts, squash courts, billiards room.*

1

VOYAGES D'ANTAN

This is a company based in Geneva that sends customers on cultural tours of the UK and Europe, combining visits to the capital cities and the countryside. Their clients are interested in art, architecture, and history. Most of the customers are over forty and children do not come on these tours. Groups are always escorted by cultural guides who research the sites of interest beforehand.

M Pierre Leroi
Voyages D'Antan
Rue St Jacques
GENEVA

Dear M Leroi

I am writing ¹*by/in/with* response ²*to/at/in* your letter of May 19 regarding suitable hotels for your four-day cultural tours of London and the UK.

The first hotel I would recommend is the _____

_____

I think that this would be particularly suitable because_____

_____

_____

The other hotel we would suggest is the _____

_____

_____

_____

³*With/By/For* reference ⁴*of/to/over* a separate matter, may I remind you that ⁵*in/with/at* accordance ⁶*to/by/with* our contract, we allow clients a 30-day credit period for invoices. Could you please let us know when we can expect the cheque for £2,926 ⁷*to/in/for* payment ⁸*of/at/for* our work for the Historic Houses Tour in March?

I look forward to hearing from you.

Yours sincerely

_____

2

Mlle du Bellay
Vacances en Famille
Rue St Michel
PARIS

Dear Mlle du Bellay

I am writing ¹*in/on/for* behalf ²*to/of/from* our
Director, Mr Slater, who has asked me to supply you
with names of two recommended hotels for your
Vacances en Famille programme.

The first one we can suggest is the _____

_____

_____

_____

_____

_____

The other hotel we can recommend is the

_____

_____

_____

_____

_____

_____

_____

³*In/On/By* view ⁴*at/with/of* the relatively high cost
of both these hotels, may I suggest that you come to
inspect them personally ⁵*in/with/by* a view ⁶*on/for/to*
ensuring that they meet your standards? ⁷*At/On/In* the
unlikely event ⁸*with/of/to* their failing to meet your
standards, we would be in a position to visit
alternatives. We are currently ⁹*by/in/with* the
process ¹⁰*to/on/of* printing our new brochure, which
will have details of a wide range of hotels
¹¹*in/with/by* addition ¹²*on/for/to* the ones listed
above, and we will send you a copy shortly.

I look forward to hearing from you.

_____

Vacances en famille

This is a French holiday
company based in Paris that
sends family groups to Britain.
Most of their clients have
young children, so it is
important for the hotels to be
able to cater for their needs,
and for there to be enough
activities for the children to do.
Customers are looking for good
value, but many of their
customers are quite wealthy
and not too worried about
price.

Exercise 4   Laura Smith has been to visit the Warton Manor Hotel on behalf of Incentive Tours. She telephones the office with a short report.

'¹Hi, Laura Smith here. I'm just phoning to give Mr Vanmeer my impressions of the Warton Manor Hotel, which I have just visited. ²On the whole, it is an excellent hotel, and it seems to be very well managed. ³I think it has a lovely atmosphere, and it will appeal to anyone who likes historic houses, but there are plenty of modern facilities too. ⁴I had an excellent meal in the restaurant and it didn't cost very much. ⁵I can't send Mr Vanmeer a full report at the moment because I've been dealing with a group from Chicago and I've been very busy, but I'm going back there next week to discuss discounts, and I'll call again when they have given me the figures. ⁶I'll be coming over to Washington next month, and I will bring their new brochure because I will have received it by then.'

Mr Vanmeer is not in the office. Imagine you are his secretary, and complete the memo to him, reporting what Laura Smith said.

M E M O

To: Mr Vanmeer

From:_____

Re: Laura Smith's visit to Warton Manor Hotel - phone call of 14 December

1 Laura Smith phoned while you were out. She said she was phoning to give you _____

_____

_____

2 She said that, on the whole, _____

_____

_____

3 She thought that it _____

_____

_____

4 She said that _____

_____

_____

5 She explained that _____

_____

_____

6 She finished by saying that _____

_____

_____

_____

Unit 12

Exercise 1

The Front Office manager is welcoming a group from Germany. Find the hidden word by writing in the missing words from the dialogue. The first one has been done for you.

MANAGER: Good afternoon. You must be Mrs Kleist from Sonnenreise.

MRS KLEIST: Yes, that's right. I'm the tour ¹___ .

MANAGER: How was your flight?

MRS KLEIST: Not bad, thank you. There was a bit of a ²___ at Frankfurt Airport, so that's why we're a little late.

MANAGER: Oh dear! Well, you'll be pleased to hear that the rooms are ready for everyone in your ³___ . Shall we fill in the check-⁴___ sheet?

MRS KLEIST: Yes. That'd be fine.

MANAGER: I've got the registration ⁵___ here, thirty-eight in all. Could you ask your party to fill them in – all we need is ⁶___ names and passport numbers.

MRS KLEIST: Right. Now, there's been a slight change. One of the people on the ⁷___ missed the flight in Frankfurt – Mr Heine. I think he might be coming later, but I haven't had time to find out yet.

MANAGER: That's OK. We'll keep the room until you find out what's happening.

MRS KLEIST: I've got the ⁸___ list here for you. It's got everyone's name on it.

MANAGER: Thanks. I'll leave a note for ⁹___ telling them you're one guest short.

MRS KLEIST: And I've got the voucher here too. Here you are.

MANAGER: Thank you very much. Right, that'll be all for the moment. If you'd like to get the registration cards ¹⁰___ in, we'll tell everyone what ¹¹___ they'll be staying in. By the way, the bar's open if anyone would like a ¹²___ while they're waiting.

MRS KLEIST: Thank you.

Exercise 2

Match the sentences in column A with their endings in column B. The first one has been done for you.

A

1 _c_ We wouldn't come here so regularly

2 __ It's a pity there's no pool. If there was,

3 __ If it snowed here regularly,

4 __ If we didn't take down everyone's details,

5 __ I would go on more of the organized excursions

6 __ If we had more groups from Japan,

7 __ If we processed everyone in a group individually,

8 __ If we didn't get large group bookings,

9 __ If we had any spare rooms with a sea view,

10 __ What difference in price would there be

B

a we would find it very difficult to make a profit.

b checking in would take a long time.

c if we didn't like it here.

d I would let you have one.

e we could go swimming.

f we would employ someone who could speak the language.

g if three of us shared a room?

h this place would make a marvellous winter resort.

i if they were a bit more interesting.

j we wouldn't know who was staying.

Exercise 3

Put the verbs in brackets into the correct tense, using **would** + infinitive or the Simple Past.

Example:
I *would help* (help) you if I *could* (can), but I'm afraid I don't have the authority to give you a discount.

a The guests _____ (not/feel) so tired if the journey from the airport _____ (not/take) such a long time.

b We haven't got any facilities for business travellers. If we _____ (have), I'm sure we _____ (make) more money in the low season.

c If the fax machine _____ (be) working, you _____ (can) send the fax from here, but I'm afraid it's out of order.

d If I _____ (be) you, I _____ (have) a word with the manager.

e   If we _____ (know) what people were
    interested in before a tour started, we _____
    _____ (be) able to make the excursions much more appealing.

f   If anyone in the group _____ (have) a
    serious medical problem or a bad accident, we _____
    _____ (fly) them back home.

g   Do you think anyone in your group _____
    _____ (be) interested if we _____
    (arrange) an evening of folk dancing?

h   If I _____ (have) the voucher, I
    _____ (give) it to you, but I have no idea
    where it is.

Exercise 4

You have been working in Reception. Tell the Manager about the
questions you have been asked, and what you said to the various guests.

Example:

MRS GRUBER: Will I be able to pay by Eurocheque?

YOU: I'll check with the Manager and let you know.

Mrs Gruber asked if she would be able to pay by Eurocheque, and I said I
would check with you and let her know.

a   MR PETERS: Can you give me a different room?

    YOU: I'll arrange it for this afternoon.

    _____

    _____

b   TOUR LEADER: Where is the passport list?

    YOU: I'm not sure. I'll ask the Manager.

    _____

    _____

c   YOU: Did everyone manage to catch the plane?

    TOUR LEADER: No, one person missed it.

    _____

    _____

d   YOU: When will you be leaving?

    TOUR LEADER: We will all be here until Monday.

    _____

    _____

Exercise 5   Fill the blanks in the following extracts with these abbreviations.

inc.   p.m.   p.p.   p.p.p.n.   P.S.   R.S.V.P.   supp.
VAT

The Manager of the Wilson Conference Centre requests the
pleasure of the company of

Mr John Smythe

for dinner at the Banqueting Hall,

Wilson Conference Centre at 6.00 1 _____ *on Sunday 18 July.*

2 _____ *(regrets only) Black tie*

Anyway, I must rush now and catch the post.

Lots of love,

Deirdre

3 _____ Hope the interview went well!

TORQUAY
PALACE
HOTEL

Prices from £45 6 _____ .
Prices based on 2 adults sharing.
Single person 7 _____ : £21.00

**'PHANTOM OF
THE OPERA'**
Tickets £20.00 each

4 _____   5 _____

I look forward to hearing from you.

Yours sincerely,

Janet Edwards

8 _____   Lawrence Rider
               Manager

Exercise 6   1   Complete the following job advertisement. Use the letters in brackets to make the missing words. The first one has been done for you.

TAILOR-MADE HOLIDAYS

RESORT REPRESENTATIVES

Seychelles — Maldives — St Lucia — Mauritius — Bali

TMH is one of the leading tour operators specializing in luxury holidays in a wide range of countries across the world. We are looking for young men and women to act as [1]*resort* (eorrst) representatives in a number of hotels [2]_____ (aabdor).

The posts [3]_____ (eilnovv) collecting clients from the airport, [4]_____ (ghinost) welcome parties, organizing social events and excursions, [5]_____ (agiiilns) with hotel staff and dealing with any day-to-day problems as they arise.

Aged between 20 and 30, the ideal [6]_____ (acddeinst) will have a mature and [7]_____ (beealnoprs) outlook, an outgoing personality, and a [8]_____ (afilr) for organization. You will need to [9]_____ (adeemnorstt) an ability to cope under [10]_____ (eeprrssu), and ideally will have held a similar [11]_____ (iinoopst) in the past. A [12]_____ (deegklnow) of French would be an [13]_____ (aaadegntv).

In return we offer a competitive [14]_____ (aalrsy), free flights, accommodation, and medical [15]_____ (aceinnrsu). Please send CVs to

Mrs Marie Clarke, TMH,
128 Grosvenor Street,
London SW1 3H.

2   Choose the correct words from the options in italics to complete the
following letter from Mary Watson, who is applying for the job of Resort
Representative. The first one has been done for you as an example.

Dear [1]*Madam/<u>Mrs Clarke</u>/Mrs Marie,*

I am writing in [2]*return/answer/reply* to your
advertisement in this month's [3]*volume/edition/
version* of the 'Hotel and Caterer' magazine
[4]*for/to/with* a Resort Representative.

[5]*As/When/Like* you will see from the enclosed
[6]*CV/CD/CA*, I have had several years [7]*knowledge/
experience/awareness* of this kind of work. After
leaving Catering College, I worked at the
Copthorne Tara Hotel as a Travel Co-ordinator,
[8]*where/when/what* I looked [9]*after/for/on* groups from
abroad. Last summer I worked in Greece [10]*as/in/like*
a Resort Representative for Cricket Holidays, and
greatly enjoyed organizing activities and events
[11]*as well as/like/in addition* being responsible for
[12]*dealing/involving/sorting* with any difficulties
the clients had.

I [13]*may/shall/would* welcome the opportunity to work
for your organization, and look forward to [14]*hear/
hearing/when I hear* from you.

Yours [15]*faithfully/hopefully/sincerely*

Mary Watson

Mary Watson

Answer Key

Unit 1

Exercise 1
a Forte Crest Hotel
b Grosvenor House Apartments
c The Waldorf

Exercise 2
1 – g	4 – h	7 – e
2 – f	5 – c	8 – d
3 – i	6 – b	9 – a

Exercise 3
a like	f enjoy
b enjoy going	g don't mind it when
c hate travelling	h love staying
d dislike it when	i don't like it when
e can't stand	

Exercise 4
1
a love it	d enjoy
b am not very fond	e hate
c am quite keen	

2
Student's own answers.

Exercise 5
a – 3	e – 1	i – 9
b – 6	f – 10	j – 5
c – 8	g – 4	k – 7
d – 2	h – 12	l – 11

Exercise 6
a – 8	f – 5
b – 2	g – 3
c – 9	h – 6
d – 4	i – 1
e – 10	j – 7

Exercise 7
1 situated	5 facilities	9 air-conditioned
2 spacious	6 informal	10 setting
3 lies	7 entertainment	11 value
4 rustic	8 furnished	12 relax

Exercise 8
1 CABINS	6 STABLES
2 SUITE	7 HOTEL
3 APARTMENT	8 SHOWER
4 COTTAGE	The hidden word is BUNGALOW.
5 CAMPSITE	

Unit 2

Exercise 1
1 telephone in my bedroom
2 TV
3 mini-bar
4 air-conditioning
5 swimming-pool
6 children are welcomed
7 play tennis
8 games room
9 special Christmas arrangements

Exercise 2
a make	made	made	f pay	paid	paid	
b go	went	gone	g know	knew	known	
c ring	rang	rung	h speak	spoke	spoken	
d fly	flew	flown	i wear	wore	worn	
e spend	spent	spent	j write	wrote	written	

Exercise 3
1 did it arrive	6 left	11 faxed
2 did you spend	7 didn't you like	12 sent
3 went	8 thought	13 booked
4 Did you have	9 did you make	
5 didn't like	10 did not write	

Exercise 4
a They have put new baths in all the bathrooms.
b They have replaced all the old beds.
c They have taken down the old wallpaper.
d They have changed all the pictures.
e They have laid new carpets.
f They have installed colour TVs in all the rooms.
g They have spent a lot of money on curtains and fabrics.
h They have built new cupboards in all the rooms.

Exercise 5
1 visited	9 have redecorated	17 has been
2 decided	10 have made	18 trained
3 were	11 have also built	19 worked
4 needed	12 have started	20 has created
5 felt	13 has introduced	21 (has) hired
6 was not	14 (has) increased	22 had
7 did not seem	15 (has) sent	23 thought
8 has changed	16 has improved	

Exercise 6
expensive	more expensive than	the most expensive
clean	cleaner than	the cleanest
good	better than	the best
cheap	cheaper than	the cheapest
interesting	more interesting than	the most interesting
bad	worse than	the worst
spacious	more spacious than	the most spacious
comfortable	more comfortable than	the most comfortable
big	bigger than	the biggest
busy	busier than	the busiest
quiet	quieter than	the quietest

Exercise 7
1 the most suitable	7 the best
2 the cheapest	8 most expensive
3 the smallest	9 most popular
4 bigger	10 larger
5 more spacious	11 quieter
6 more expensive	

Exercise 8
a play-room	e safety rail
b nappy-changing	f wheelchair access
c courtesy bus	g king-size
d resident nurse	h stair lift

Unit 3

Exercise 1
1 – d	4 – b	7 – e
2 – a	5 – g	8 – c
3 – h	6 – i	9 – f

Exercise 2
1
1 must
2 mustn't
3 don't have to
4 must
5 must
6 must
7 don't have to

2
1 have to
2 don't have to
3 don't have to
4 have to
5 have to
6 shouldn't
7 shouldn't

3
1 should
2 should
3 don't have to
4 mustn't
5 should
6 should
7 should
8 shouldn't

4
Passage 1: chambermaid
Passage 2: concierge
Passage 3: barman/barmaid

Exercise 3

1
a enthusiastic
b experience
c friendly
d ability
e relevant
f permanent
g responsibility
h available
i awareness
j suitable

2
a suitable
b relevant
c aware
d ability
e friendly
f experience
g responsible
h available
i permanent

Exercise 4

a turnover rate
b winter quarter
c personal touch
d heavy workload
e kitchen garden
f regular clientele
g permanent staff
h twelve-bedroomed

Exercise 5

1 conference
2 Golf
3 National
4 challenging
5 professional
6 communication
7 essential
8 minimum
9 experience
10 competitive
11 opportunity
12 Personnel

Exercise 6

1 Writing
2 post
3 placed
4 care
5 opportunity
6 enclosed
7 leaving
8 For
9 as
10 valuable
11 with
12 knowledge
13 little
14 available
15 forward
16 hearing
17 sincerely

Exercise 7

1 PURCHASING
2 PERSONNEL
3 PORTER
4 ACCOUNTS
5 CHAMBERMAID
6 CONCIERGE
7 FRONT
8 MANAGER
9 CHEF
10 RECEPTIONIST
11 MAINTENANCE
12 HOUSEKEEPER

The hidden word is APPOINTMENTS.

Unit 4

Exercise 1

a – 12
b – 2
c – 8
d – 3
e – 6
f – 10
g – 5
h – 9
i – 13
j – 1
k – 11
l – 7
m – 4
n – 14

Exercise 2

Name	Henry Box
Arrival date	11th May
No. of nights	2
Room type	Double
Company/Individual	Individual
Stayed before	No
Method of payment	American Express
Credit card no.	8773 457 238 5549
Address	30 Lime Walk, Slough
Reservation no.	P227

Exercise 3

a Yes, it is.
b Yes, I do.
c Yes, I do.
d Yes, there is.
e No, I haven't.
f No, they aren't.
g No, they haven't.
h Yes, you may.
i No, I didn't.
j Yes, I have.

Exercise 4

a Yes, they did.
b No, they didn't.
c No, they weren't.
d No, they didn't.
e Yes, it did.
f No, it wasn't.
g No, they didn't.
h Yes, they could.
i No, it wasn't.
j Yes, it did.

Peter stayed at the Granada.
The Smiths stayed at the Seville.
Mary stayed at the Alhambra.

Exercise 5

1 – d
2 – f
3 – b
4 – h
5 – i
6 – g
7 – j
8 – e
9 – a
10 – c

Exercise 6

1 Can
2 have
3 Hold
4 put
5 I'm afraid
6 hold
7 fine
8 ringing
9 speaking
10 this is
11 do
12 sorry
13 bad
14 of course
15 grateful
16 confirm
17 Certainly
18 You're

Exercise 7

1 MERGE
2 SCREEN
3 WINDOWS
4 PROCESSOR
5 FORMAT
6 DATA
7 ACCESS
8 PASSWORD
9 NETWORK
10 SOFTWARE

Exercise 8

1
1 reserve
2 following
3 Executive
4 single
5 en-suite
6 availability
7 details
8 including
9 discount
10 Regards

2
Example answer

Date: 24 May
From: Reservations
To: Imperial Chemicals
Attention: Miranda Smith, Marketing and Promotions

Thank you for your booking for Mr Henry Green and Miss Caroline Lamb. I have reserved the rooms as you requested.

Prices for the Executive rooms + half-board, taxes and service charges are normally £165 p.p. per night. Standard rooms + half-board, taxes and service charges are £85 p.p. per night.

The total price including your discount of 10% will be £526.50.

Regards

Unit 5

Exercise 1

1 – d
2 – h
3 – j
4 – f
5 – i
6 – c
7 – a
8 – g
9 – e
10 – b

Exercise 2

a British
b American
c American
d British
e American
f British
g British
h American
i British
j American

Exercise 3

A broccoli, peas, leeks
B apple, béchamel, tartare
C lyonnaise, rösti, sauté
D haddock, plaice, salmon
E ham, pork, veal

Exercise 4

1

a They're a variety of shellfish that look like lobsters, but are much smaller.
b They're a kind of sweet made with chocolate, eggs and liqueur.
c It's a kind of meat that comes from young calves.
d They're thinly sliced potatoes that are baked with garlic and cream.
e It's a kind of sauce made with milk, vanilla, eggs and sugar.
f It's a very light dish made with egg whites, and baked in the oven.
g It's a kind of fish that is quite large and has pink flesh.
h It's a kind of vegetable with a white stem and a green top.

2

Student's own answers.

Exercise 5

Example answers

a I'll put it on your account.
b I'll get you a new one.
c I'll call a taxi for you.
d I'll put them in the safe for you.
e I'll look it up in the telephone directory.

Exercise 6

1 am going to buy	6 I'll ring
2 are you going to buy	7 I'll give
3 am going to get	8 are going to see
4 I'll have	9 I'll let
5 I'll get	

Exercise 7

1 Would you like a table for two?
2 Would you like a table in the corner?
3 Would you like to order an aperitif?
4 Here is the menu and the wine list.
5 Are you ready to order now?
6 What would you like as a starter?
7 What would you like to follow?
8 How would you like your steaks done?
9 Would you like to order some wine with your meal?
10 I'll get one right away.

Exercise 8

Example answers

1

CONCIERGE: Mr Hertz (284) wants to know about the Acropolis excursion tomorrow. What happens? How much does it cost? Please ring him.

2

MR JOHN HARVEY (635): Mr Peter Franks rang. He'll call back later.

Unit 6

Exercise 1

1 check out	7 There's	13 would
2 have	8 for	14 pay
3 I'll	9 I'll	15 accept
4 away	10 worry	16 don't you
5 Here you are	11 must	17 we do
6 check	12 seems	

Exercise 2

1

1 – b	3 – e	5 – f
2 – d	4 – c	6 – a

2

a One hundred and twenty-one dollars and twenty-five cents times four is four hundred and eighty-five dollars.
b Ninety cents times three is two dollars and seventy cents.
c One hundred pounds at one point six two four dollars to the pound is one hundred and sixty-two dollars and forty cents.
d Two hundred dollars less/minus fifteen per cent is one hundred and seventy dollars.
e Twelve dollars divided by four comes to three dollars each.

Exercise 3

1 RATES	4 DEPOSIT	7 RECEIPT	10 NOTES
2 VOUCHER	5 ADVANCE	8 CHEQUE	
3 CREDIT	6 CASH	9 OUT	

The hidden word is EUROCHEQUE.

Exercise 4

1

a are	c was	e has been	g will be
b is being	d was being	f had been	

2

a were given a 15% discount.
b is being emptied for maintenance.
c are asked to check out by 12.00.
d will be returned by 9 a.m. the following morning.
e was included in the bill.
f hasn't this bill been paid yet?
g luggage was being brought down.

Exercise 5

1 In order to prevent credit card fraud, the following procedures must be followed.
2 Firstly, the expiry date of the card must be checked.
3 If the date is still valid, an authorization code should be obtained from the credit card company.
4 The voucher should be filled in and signed in the presence of the employee.
5 The signatures on the card and the voucher should be compared.
6 Finally, if the signatures match, the card and the top copy of the voucher should be returned to the customer.

1 Basically, what you have to do is this.
2 First of all, make sure that the card isn't out of date.
3 If it's still valid, you phone the credit card company for an authorization number.
4 Then you fill in the voucher and ask them to sign it while you are looking.
5 When they've signed it, check that the signatures are the same.
6 If they are, you give them back their card and the top sheet of the voucher, and that's it.

Exercise 6

The most suitable suite is the Derwent.

1 five	5 £50	9 10%
2 February 10th	6 English breakfast	10 10%
3 Derwent	7 dinner	11 five
4 balcony	8 February	12 £200

1 Mr M Hayward
2 10 Hollybush Lane, Elsfield, OXON
3 OX2 3AU
4 *Student's own invention*
5 two
6 Derwent
7 five
8 10 February
9 15 February
10 £50
11 M Hayward
12 *Student's own invention*

Unit 7

Exercise 1

1B → 9B → 17B → 7B → 14 → 3
1C → 18B → 19A → 4C → 5 → 2

Exercise 2

a The plug in 213 has been mended.
b The kettle in 215 hasn't been replaced.
c The red wine stain on the carpet in 316 hasn't been cleaned up.
d The bedcovers in 302 have been changed.
e The bins in the corridor on the third floor have been emptied.
f The leaking tap in 403 hasn't been repaired.
g The cot hasn't been put in 416.
h The air-conditioning in 500 has been adjusted.

Exercise 3

Example answers

a She shouldn't have shouted at the customer.
b She should have corrected the mistake immediately.
c He shouldn't have been so rude.
d He should have been more attentive.
e He shouldn't have sent it to the dining-room if it was badly cooked.
f He should have cooked it better.
g She should have worked harder.
h She shouldn't have made so many mistakes.
i He shouldn't have lost the passport.
j He should have put it in the safe.

Exercise 4

a absolutely		f terribly	
b very		g absolutely	
c good		h extremely	
d bad		i dirty	
e disgusting		j enormous	

Exercise 5

1 Thank you for	7 I can assure you
2 I was sorry to hear	8 As a sign of our concern
3 I would like to point out	9 I hope
4 adequate notice	10 Please accept
5 Unfortunately	11 sincerely
6 in advance	

Unit 8

Exercise 1

a Archery, fencing, clay pigeon shooting, horse riding, windsurfing.
b Clay pigeon shooting, fencing.
c Archery, clay pigeon shooting, horse riding.
d £9.60, for one parent, one child; £15.35, for two parents, one child.
e Fencing (Parent and Child Musketeer), beginners' riding lessons, ten-pin bowling.
f Fencing, horse riding, windsurfing.
g £8.60 (£5.60 for two hours plus £3 for launch of private board).
h Ten-pin bowling.
i Ten-pin bowling (£8.35 for 45 minutes) or fast trek horse riding (£14.30 for 1 hour and 30 minutes).

Exercise 2

1 decides	9 is
2 must	10 will have
3 goes	11 decides
4 will get back	12 will let you know
5 chooses	13 make
6 won't/will not return	14 wants
7 will she get back	15 won't/will not get
8 goes	16 don't/do not book

Exercise 3

Example answers

a If you ring room service, they will send breakfast to your room.
b If you pay cash, you will get 10% discount.
c If you use this cream, you will be completely protected against the sun.
d If you aren't sixteen, you can't go to the disco.
e If you have a valid guarantee card, you can pay by cheque.
f If you go to the airport in the courtesy coach, it will take thirty-five minutes.
g If you want to go on the Santorini tour, you must book early.
h If you leave valuables in your room, they will be stolen.

Exercise 4

Student's own answers, beginning with:

a Why don't you . . .
b If I were you, I'd . . .
c You could always . . .

Exercise 5

a 5	c 1	e 4	g 2
b 3	d 7	f 6	h 8

Exercise 6

1 WAIVER	4 MANUAL	7 TANK
2 RENTAL	5 PARTY	8 LICENCE
3 SEATS	6 TAXES	9 MILEAGE

The hidden word is INSURANCE.

Unit 9

Exercise 1

a Like	c Unlike	e just as	g whereas
b Just as	d whereas	f Like	h Unlike

Exercise 2

a How long have you been living there?
b How long have you been staying here?
c How long have you been working for them?
d How long has she been waiting for me?
e How long have you been coming here?
f How long have you been having conferences here?

Exercise 3

a No, I've been coming here for years.
b No, I've been working here since last September.
c Thank you, I've been studying it for five years.
d No, we've been looking after them for a long time.
e He hasn't been doing the job for very long.
f We've been growing all our own herbs since the hotel opened.

Exercise 4

1 have been waiting	6 have dealt
2 have rung	7 have had
3 has used	8 have paid
4 have had	9 have written
5 have been coming	10 has been trying

Exercise 5

1

a 5	c 1	e 4
b 3	d 6	f 2

2

a False.	c True.	e True.	g True.
b False.	d True.	f False.	h True.

Exercise 6

Student's own answers.

Exercise 7

1 SECRETARIAL	6 MEETING
2 TELETEXT	7 STATIONERY
3 OVERHEAD	8 VIPS
4 SCREEN	9 PRINTER
5 COMPUTER	

The hidden word is EXECUTIVE.

Unit 10

Exercise 1

1 run	7 style	13 expecting
2 requirements	8 workshop	14 exact
3 suitable	9 classroom	15 think of
4 giving	10 exhibition	16 space
5 delegates	11 square	
6 seating	12 possibilities	

Exercise 2

a the Stour Room
b the Purbeck Bar
c the President's Suite
d the Purbeck Lounge
e the Bourne Lounge

Exercise 3

Example answers

The Telford Room is a square room sixteen metres by sixteen. It can be used for exhibitions, meetings, and wedding receptions. It has a seating capacity of 215 in theatre-style and 220 in reception-style. It has air-conditioning, a public address system, a lectern, and a 35mm projector. It also has large windows providing natural daylight, and a stage area.

The Tudor Hall is a large conference room measuring 43 metres by 46 metres, with a smaller room measuring eight metres by five adjoining it. It is used for major international conferences and can seat 3900 people (in theatre-style only). The equipment includes a projection room, a screen, and simultaneous translation facilities. A bar, coffee lounge and toilets are situated in the adjoining room.

Exercise 4

Example answers

a A corkscrew is used for getting the cork out of a bottle.
b A lectern is used for holding the speaker's notes while he or she is speaking.
c A transparency is used with an overhead projector for showing information such as graphs, charts, etc.
d An Autocue is like a transparent television screen and is used, instead of notes, for reminding the speaker of what he or she has to say.
e A flip-chart is a block of large sheets of paper on a stand and is used for the speaker to write on while he or she is speaking.
f A bottle opener is used for taking the caps off bottles.
g An OHP marker is used for writing on a transparent sheet for showing on an OHP projector.
h A stapler is used for fastening pieces of paper together.

Exercise 5

1 acres	8 but	15 provided
2 example	9 offers	16 team
3 has	10 facilities	17 including
4 to	11 chance	18 advantage
5 makes	12 pool	19 such
6 venue	13 some	20 style
7 soon	14 whether	21 success

Exercise 6

Example answer

I am writing to introduce Hollway House, the best conference centre in London. Please find enclosed our brochure which explains why we believe Hollway House will suit your requirements perfectly.

You will find Hollway House a perfect venue for conferences, training courses, etc. We provide the very latest facilities in an atmosphere of peaceful elegance. We are proud of our excellent cuisine and attentive service, which we believe is the best in the country.

Our prices are very competitive and many extras are included in the 24-hour delegate rate. We provide all the necessary equipment, secretarial support, mineral water and daily newspapers with no additional charge. We believe we offer excellent value for money.

We would be pleased to make arrangments for you to visit Hollway House to view our facilities. If you require any further information, please do not hesitate to contact me. We look forward to hearing from you.

Unit 11

Exercise 1

1 will be setting off	7 will be spending
2 will be sailing	8 will be going on
3 will be arriving	9 will be coming
4 will be staying	10 will be leaving
5 will be using	11 will be stopping
6 will be having	12 will be boarding

Exercise 2

a will have completed	f will have left
b will still be going round	g will be sitting
c will be sending	h won't/will not have had
d will be going	i will have made
e won't/will not have finished	j will be seeing

Exercise 3

1

1 in
2 to

The first hotel I would recommend is the Thornbury Castle. I think this would be particularly suitable because the hotel is of great historical and architectural interest, the accommodation is very comfortable, and no children under 12 years are allowed.

The other hotel we would suggest is the Bloomsbury, in an area of London associated for a long time with Britain's greatest writers, artists, and musicians, and very close to the British Museum, Covent Garden Opera House, and London's finest art galleries.

3 With	5 in	7 in	
4 to	6 with	8 for	

2

1 on   2 of

The first one we can suggest is the Woolley Grange hotel near Bradford-on-Avon. Children are particularly welcome in this hotel, and there is a range of facilities for them – riding, swimming, dry skiing, etc. The hotel is a Jacobean manor house and the bedrooms are furnished with antiques.

The other hotel we can recommend is the Imperial, in Torquay. This was established in 1866 and is one of Britain's leading resort hotels. There are baby-listening and baby-sitting facilities, and also many attractions for children, such as activity programmes and a model village, as well as sports facilities.

3 In	6 to	9 in	12 to
4 of	7 In	10 of	
5 with	8 of	11 in	

Exercise 4

1 Laura Smith phoned while you were out. She said she was phoning to give you her impressions of the Warton Manor Hotel, which she had just visited.
2 She said that, on the whole, it was an excellent hotel, and it seemed to be very well managed.
3 She thought that it had a lovely atmosphere, and it would appeal to anyone who liked historic houses, but there were plenty of modern facilities too.
4 She said that she had had an excellent meal in the restaurant and it hadn't cost very much.
5 She explained that she couldn't send you a full report because she had been dealing with a group from Chicago and she had been very busy, but she was going back there next week to discuss discounts, and she would call again when they had given her the figures.
6 She finished by saying that she would be coming over to Washington next month, and she would bring their new brochure because she would have received it by then.

Unit 12

Exercise 1

1 LEADER	4 IN	7 TOUR	10 FILLED
2 DELAY	5 CARDS	8 PASSPORT	11 ROOMS
3 GROUP	6 THEIR	9 RECEPTION	12 DRINK

The hidden word is REGISTRATION.

Exercise 2

1 – c	4 – j	7 – b	10 – g
2 – e	5 – i	8 – a	
3 – h	6 – f	9 – d	

Exercise 3

a would not feel … did not take	e knew … would be
b had … would make	f had … would fly
c was … could	g would be … arranged
d were … would have	h had … would give

Exercise 4

a Mr Peters asked if we/I could give him a different room, and I said I would arrange it for this afternoon.
b The tour leader asked where the passport list was, and I said I wasn't sure but I would ask the manager.
c I asked the tour leader if everyone had managed to catch the plane, and she said that one person had missed it.
d I asked the tour leader when they would be leaving, and she said they would all be here until Monday.

Exercise 5

1 p.m.	3 P.S.	5 VAT	7 supp.
2 R.S.V.P.	4 inc.	6 p.p.p.n.	8 p.p.

Exercise 6

1

1 resort	6 candidates	11 position
2 abroad	7 personable	12 knowledge
3 involve	8 flair	13 advantage
4 hosting	9 demonstrate	14 salary
5 liaising	10 pressure	15 insurance

2

1 Mrs Clarke	6 CV	11 as well as
2 reply	7 experience	12 dealing
3 edition	8 where	13 would
4 for	9 after	14 hearing
5 As	10 as	15 sincerely